Shonen Knife's
Happy Hour

33 1/3 Global

33 1/3 Global, a series related to but independent from **33 1/3**, takes the format of the original series of short, music-based books and brings the focus to music throughout the world. With initial volumes focusing on Japanese and Brazilian music, the series will also include volumes on the popular music of Australia/Oceania, Europe, Africa, the Middle East, and more.

33 1/3 Japan

Series Editor: Noriko Manabe

Spanning a range of artists and genres—from the 1960s rock of Happy End to technopop band Yellow Magic Orchestra, the Shibuya-kei of Cornelius, classic anime series *Cowboy Bebop*, J-Pop/EDM hybrid Perfume, and vocaloid star Hatsune Miku—**33 1/3 Japan** is a series devoted to in-depth examination of Japanese albums of the twentieth and twenty-first centuries.

Published Titles:
Supercell's *Supercell* by Keisuke Yamada
Yoko Kanno's *Cowboy Bebop Soundtrack* by Rose Bridges
Perfume's *Game* by Patrick St. Michel
AKB48 by Patrick W. Galbraith and Jason G. Karlin
Cornelius's *Fantasma* by Martin Roberts
Joe Hisaishi's *My Neighbor Totoro: Soundtrack* by Kunio Hara
Shonen Knife's *Happy Hour* by Brooke McCorkle Okazaki
Nenes' *Koza Dabasa* by Henry Johnson

33 1/3 Brazil

Series Editor: Jason Stanyek

Covering the genres of samba, tropicália, rock, hip-hop, forró, bossa nova, heavy metal, and funk, among others, **33 1/3 Brazil** is a series devoted to in-depth examination of the most important Brazilian albums of the twentieth and twenty-first centuries.

Published Titles:
Caetano Veloso's *A Foreign Sound* by Barbara Browning
Tim Maia's *Tim Maia Racional Vols. 1 &2* by Allen Thayer
João Gilberto and Stan Getz's *Getz/Gilberto* by Brian McCann
Dona Ivone Lara's *Sorriso Negro* by Mila Burns
Gilberto Gil's *Refazenda* by Marc A. Hertzman
Milton Nascimento and Lô Borges's *The Corner Club* by Jonathon Grasse

Forthcoming titles:
Racionais MCs' *Sobrevivendo no Inferno* by Marília Gessa
    and Derek Pardue
Jorge Ben Jor's *África Brasil* by Frederick J. Moehn
Naná Vasconcelos's *Saudades* by Daniel B. Sharp

33 1/3 Europe

Series Editor: Fabian Holt
Spanning a range of artists and genres, **33 1/3 Europe** offers engaging accounts of popular and culturally significant albums of Continental Europe and the North Atlantic from the twentieth and twenty-first centuries.

Published Titles:
Darkthrone's *A Blaze in the Northern Sky* by Ross Hagen
Ivo Papasov's *Balkanology* by Carol Silverman

Forthcoming Titles:
Modeselektor's *Happy Birthday* by Sean Nye
Various Artists' *DJs do Guetto* by Richard Elliott
Bea Playa's *I'll Be Your Plaything* by Anna Szemere and András Rónai
Heiner Müller and Heiner Goebbels's *Wolokolamsker Chaussee*
    by Philip V. Bohlman
Los Rodriguez's *Sin Documentos* by Fernán del Val and Héctor Fouce
Mercyful Fate's *Don't Break the Oath* by Henrik Marstal
Massada's *Astaganaga* by Lutgard Mutsaers

Nuovo Canzoniere's *Bella Ciao* by Jacopo Tomatis
Czesław Niemen's *Niemen Enigmatic* by Ewa Mazierska and Mariusz Gradowski
Amália Rodrigues's *Live at the Olympia* by Lilla Ellen Gray
Ardit Gjebrea's *Projekt Jon* by Nicholas Tochka
Vopli Vidopliassova's *Tantsi* by Maria Sonevytsky
Édith Piaf's *Recital 1961* by David Looseley

Shonen Knife's *Happy Hour*

Food, Gender, Rock and Roll

Brooke McCorkle Okazaki

Noriko Manabe, Series Editor

BLOOMSBURY ACADEMIC
NEW YORK • LONDON • OXFORD • NEW DELHI • SYDNEY

BLOOMSBURY ACADEMIC
Bloomsbury Publishing Inc
1385 Broadway, New York, NY 10018, USA
50 Bedford Square, London, WC1B 3DP, UK
29 Earlsfort Terrace, Dublin 2, Ireland

BLOOMSBURY, BLOOMSBURY ACADEMIC and the Diana logo are
trademarks of Bloomsbury Publishing Plc

First published in the United States of America 2021
Reprinted 2021

Copyright © Brooke McCorkle Okazaki, 2021

For legal purposes the Acknowledgments on p. xi constitute
an extension of this copyright page.

Cover design: Louise Dugdale

All rights reserved. No part of this publication may be reproduced or
transmitted in any form or by any means, electronic or mechanical,
including photocopying, recording, or any information storage or retrieval
system, without prior permission in writing from the publishers.

Bloomsbury Publishing Inc does not have any control over, or
responsibility for, any third-party websites referred to or in this book.
All internet addresses given in this book were correct at the time of going
to press. The author and publisher regret any inconvenience caused if
addresses have changed or sites have ceased to exist, but can accept
no responsibility for any such changes.

Library of Congress Cataloging-in-Publication Data
Names: Okazaki, Brooke McCorkle, 1980- author.
Title: Shonen Knife's Happy hour: food, gender, rock and roll /
Brooke McCorkle Okazaki.
Description: New York City: Bloomsbury Academic, 2021. |
Series: 33 1/3 Japan | Includes bibliographical references and index. |
Summary: "Happy Hour, filled with pop punk songs about food,
encapsulates the international allure of the all-female punk trio from
Osaka, Japan"– Provided by publisher.
Identifiers: LCCN 2020036718 (print) | LCCN 2020036719 (ebook) |
ISBN 9781501347948 (paperback) | ISBN 9781501347962 (epub) |
ISBN 9781501347979 (pdf)
Subjects: LCSH: Shonen Knife (Musical group). Happy hour. | Punk rock
music–Japan–History and criticism. | Rock music–Japan–History and
criticism. | Food in music.
Classification: LCC ML421.S503 O56 2021 (print) | LCC ML421.S503
(ebook) | DDC 782.42166092/2 [B]–dc23
LC record available at https://lccn.loc.gov/2020036718
LC ebook record available at https://lccn.loc.gov/2020036719

ISBN: HB: 978-1-5013-4795-5
PB: 978-1-5013-4794-8
ePDF: 978-1-5013-4797-9
eBook: 978-1-5013-4796-2

Series: $33\frac{1}{3}$ Europe

Typeset by Deanta Global Publishing Services, Chennai, India
Printed and bound in Great Britain

In memory of Billie Jean Birdwell, who taught me to cook with love

Contents

List of Illustrations x
Acknowledgments xi
Preface xiv

Introduction: *Itadakimasu!* (Let's Eat!) 1

1 **Girl Bands and *Josei* Rock, 1950s–1980s** 13

2 **Food, Gender, and Music in Postwar Japan** 27

3 **Shonen Knife's Songs in the Key of Food** 45

4 ***Konnichiwa!*: An Introduction to *Happy Hour* (1998) and Its Cover Art** 65

5 ***Happy Hour:* Food, Music, and Transnational Flow** 73

6 **The Delicious Banality of "Banana Chips"** 87

7 **Sweet Candy Power: Shonen Knife's *Josei* Rock Legacy** 103

Notes 127
Bibliography 138
Selected Discography 148
Index 152

Illustrations

Images

0.1 The Powerpuff Girls: Blossom, Bubbles, and Buttercup perform as a three-piece rock band in the music video for Shonen Knife's "Buttercup (I'm a Super Girl)" 2

0.2 The original Shonen Knife lineup from 1981 to 1999 4

4.1 Nara Yoshitomo's sketch for the cover of *Happy Hour* 72

6.1 Screen capture from the "Banana Chips" music video 96

7.1 Screen capture from "After Making Love With Me, You Eat Your Wife's Meal!" music video by Otoboke Beaver 114

7.2 Screen capture from the postlude to "After Making Love With Me, You Eat Your Wife's Meal!" music video by Otoboke Beaver 115

7.3 Screen capture from the "Sweet Candy Power" music video by Shonen Knife 121

7.4 Shonen Knife rocks out at a show in Denver, Colorado during their Sweet Candy Power Tour 123

7.5 Shonen Knife wraps up a hard-rocking live show in Denver, Colorado, during their Sweet Candy Power Tour 125

Tables

2.1 Timeline of Shonen Knife's Songs about Food 28

6.1 Chart Outlining Time Codes, Images, and Musical Descriptions for the "Banana Chips" Music Video 97

Acknowledgments

This book is the product of the time and support I received from many people. I thank Shonen Knife members Yamano Naoko, Yamano Atsuko, Kawano Risa; the members of Brinky in addition to Risa, Kawano Maki, Kawano Kenji, Kawano Rina; and the members of KCollectors—Kyoko, Mamiko, and Tama-chan—for generously agreeing to speak with me. I thank Shonen Knife's manager Shibata Atsushi for help arranging my interview with Naoko and gaining access to images of the band. I am grateful to Naoko for also kindly designing this book's cover art and providing important details about the band's career. Many thanks to Shannon Bailey who shared her amazing photographs of Shonen Knife that appear in this book.

I developed the idea for a book about Shonen Knife during my college days and want to express my gratitude to professors Carolyn Abbate, Carol Muller, Tim Rommen, Ayako Kano, Linda Chance, Frank Chance, Elyssa Faison, Yoshiko Fukushima, and Michael Lee for shaping my various thoughts on music, gender, and Japanese culture. I am indebted to Sarah Laursen and Masa Takahashi at Middlebury College for inviting me to share my early work on Nara Yoshitomo and Shonen Knife with their students and to the Middlebury students themselves for their attention and insights. My colleagues at Carleton College kindly supported this endeavor and I am extremely grateful to them for their kindness.

My mom, Sharon McCorkle, tolerated my loud music in high school and supported my interest in playing bass. Brian Vivier and Lisa Stout introduced me to a wide variety of music both from Japan and elsewhere, and encouraged me to "bring the rock" to all aspects of life, for which I am thankful. Nate Olmsted opened my ears to 1970s rock. Fellow Therogy band members John Thomas, Chase Spivey, and Ben Lindesmith were excellent musical collaborators and playing with them transformed the way I think about rock music. Sean Rhoads shaped my thoughts on modern Japanese cultural history and Ōnishi Yuki enlightened me on Japanese popular music prior to the Second World War. Thanks to Rob Fairbanks, I developed a strong interest in women-led rock groups like the Go-Go's, which led me to explore similar bands in Japan.

Kondō Hiroaki, Okazaki Michiko, and fellow members of Osaka's Jazzy Dream Band welcomed me into the performance world and shared their thoughts on *kayōkyoku* with me. Kōzō Ōta and David Watkins generously introduced me to various aspects of Japan's music scene. The fans of Shonen Knife and participants on various social networks kindly provided valuable observations. I am especially grateful to Matthew Gaunt and Jeff Clayton for their help. George "Ojisan" Handlon, longtime Shonen Knife fan and editor of *The Shonen Knife Nexus*, shared with me not only his knowledge but also several rare historical documents related to Shonen Knife. I am honored to have benefited from his generosity.

I am indebted to 33 ⅓ Japan series editor Noriko Manabe, who supported this project over the last three years, and to Leah Babb-Rosenfeld, senior editor at Bloomsbury, for her kindness and patience. I also thank the anonymous reviewers for their helpful comments. I am grateful to fellow 33 ⅓ Japan author Kunio Hara; without his input and encouragement, I could not have completed this project. Finally, I thank my partner Okazaki Yūsuke. He helped me learn more about the Tokyo and Osaka rock worlds of the past and present, checked my Japanese translations, and provided emotional support in the form of delicious homemade meals during the writing and editing of this book.

Preface

Throughout this book, Japanese names are written with family names preceding given names, unless the individual is Japanese American or their career is primarily in the English-speaking world. I refer to the members of Shonen Knife by their first names, as is common among fans. Unless specified, all translations are by the author. This book employs the modified Hepburn system in regard to Japanese names and words aside from those that frequently appear in the English language, such as Tokyo and Osaka. I also omit the diacritic on "Shonen Knife" per the band's preferences. While the correct Hepburn transliteration is "Atchan," many English-language sites use "Attchan." As a result, the book follows the latter form when discussing the album. I have curated a YouTube playlist that complements this book and can be found under the same title. Warning: this book may incite hunger.

Introduction
Itadakimasu! (Let's Eat!)

July 2000, USA:

I sit on the carpet of the living room, gazing up at the glowing screen of a Sony tube television. Like any dedicated geek at the turn of the millennium, I maintain a steady diet of American and Japanese cartoons that air on Cartoon Network. Among my favorites is Craig McCracken's The Powerpuff Girls. *The show stars sisters Blossom, Bubbles, and Buttercup, superheroes created by a well-meaning scientist who accidentally added Chemical X to the quintessential ingredients of what little girls are made of: "sugar, spice, and everything nice." The result of the experiment gone awry was a trio of cute, cool doll-like girls who also know how to kick ass. One night, during a commercial break, a music video promoting* The Powerpuff Girls *animated show blares from the speakers. The pint-size superheroes zip across the screen, beating up monsters while psychedelic images swirl in the background. In one shot, the sisters perform as a rock-and-roll three-piece (see Image 0.1).*

The song begins as an overdriven guitar solo in peppy major key blasts from the television; drums and bass soon kick in. A slightly accented female voice enters, singing about fighting bad guys and never giving up. During the chorus, a futuristic synthesizer emerges from the texture as the singer declares, "You

Image 0.1 *The Powerpuff Girls: Blossom, Bubbles, and Buttercup perform as a three-piece rock band in the music video for Shonen Knife's "Buttercup (I'm a Super Girl)."*

know I'm a super girl, yes, I'm a punky girl, I never say die, no one can stop me 'cause I like to fight!" After the two-and-a-half-minute music video, information about the tune pops up on the screen. The song: "Buttercup (I'm a Supergirl)" by the band Shonen Knife.

* * *

I was smitten. As a young female punk-hippie bass player from Oklahoma, USA, I found a lot to admire in Shonen Knife's music. I listened to other female rockers—Pat Benatar, Kim Gordon, the Breeders, Blondie, the Go-Go's—but something about Shonen Knife stood out. Like Blossom, Bubbles, and Buttercup, the singer and her bandmates seemed cute and cool, happy and tough. Their sound was sugar, spice, and everything nice, with an added zing of something akin to the mysterious Chemical X. Shonen Knife was the musical version of my beloved cute cartoon champions. I had to learn more about these women from Japan who knew how to rock hard and still convey a sense of fizzy fun.

On December 29, 1981, Yamano Naoko, a young woman from Osaka—Japan's second largest city, traditionally a commercial center—decided to form a rock-and-roll band. Naoko grew up listening to Group Sounds, a Beatles-inspired genre of 1960s rock centered on the electric guitar (Bourdaghs 2012: 113–58). Yet she did not decide to start a band until the day she heard the Ramones on the radio. Naoko recounts the tale in the band's song "Ramones Forever," a cheerful track in the vein of the legendary punk heroes' style on *Fun! Fun! Fun!* (2010).[1] Naoko would play guitar and sing. She recruited her younger sister Yamano Atsuko to play drums (at early rehearsals phone books substituted for a drum set), and their friend Nakatani Michie would sit in on bass guitar and vocals.[2] The band was complete and by March 14, 1982, they were playing live shows.[3] In a 1993 interview with *Rolling Stone* magazine, Naoko explained the origins of Shonen Knife's name, which was inspired by a brand of pocketknife for children. "*Shōnen* means boy and is a cute word," she related, "and knife is a sharp word. I like mixing the two" (Wild 1993). To be more specific, *shōnen* typically refers to boys from around the ages of ten to fifteen. The term is also a marketing category, particularly when it comes to pop-culture products like manga and anime. *Naifu*, however, is a loanword from English. The band's selection of Shonen Knife as a name signals an engagement with the local and global as well as a mixture of cute with the cutting edge (see Image 0.2).

In the days before YouTube, finding music of Shonen Knife was no easy task, but I managed to track down some American releases. By the time of their music video for the

Image 0.2 *The original Shonen Knife lineup from 1981 to 1999. Left to right: Nakatani Michie, Yamano Atsuko, Yamano Naoko (Photo by Niels van Iperen/Getty Images).*

Powerpuff promotion, Shonen Knife already had a small but avid group of fans internationally (Craig McCracken among them). Sub Pop (the Seattle-based record company that represented Nirvana and many other indie bands) had promoted a 1986 compilation album, *Sub Pop 100*, featuring Shonen Knife. Thanks to this, the band achieved a degree of popularity in the United States in the late 1980s and early 1990s and garnered devoted fans like Nirvana's Kurt Cobain and Sonic Youth's Thurston Moore.[4] Cobain loved Shonen Knife's optimistic sound so much that he invited them to open for Nirvana on a U.K. tour in 1991.

The band's first American gig was with Thurston Moore in Los Angeles in 1989. Later that year, various artists including Sonic Youth, Red Kross, and L7 released a Shonen Knife cover album called *Every Band Has a Shonen Knife Who Loves Them* (1989). Moore appeared as a guest guitarist on the track "Butterfly Boy" from Shonen Knife's 1994 album *Rock Animals*, a deceptively intricate alternative rock song with heavily overdriven guitar, and instrumental and vocal bridges along with winsome lyrics. He later provided a remix of the song "Cannibal Papaya" (Hitokui Papaya) for the album *Supermix* (1992). Another alternative-grunge track of *Rock Animals*, "Tomato Head," gained acclaim thanks to a music video that circulated on MTV. In 1994, the band played at the Lollapalooza alternative rock festival, acquiring even more media attention and fans in the United States.

Because of this success abroad and in a nod to Japanese rock history more generally, the band regularly sings in English. Part of this might have had to do with the popularity of English loanwords in the Japanese language and the history of cultural exchange between Japan and English-speaking countries. Japanese popular musicians have long incorporated English into their lyrics, and Shonen Knife is no exception. The band has recorded several albums in both Japanese and English, and many received international distribution.

However, as of 2020, some of Shonen Knife's recordings are difficult to access even in Japan; for many connoisseurs, though, the challenge of acquiring them is part of the fun. Devotees around the world follow band members of the past and present on Instagram and Twitter, participate in Facebook fan pages, and maintain websites enshrining Shonen Knife and their accomplishments. Shonen Knife's global success has been going strong for around forty years and counting. With occasional changes in membership, the band survived Japan's decadent 1980s, the burst of the economic bubble in the 1990s, and the extended recession that followed. Shonen Knife continues to perform and record regularly today. In 2019, they wrapped up a months-long *Sweet Candy Power* tour across North America, the United Kingdom, and Australia. There is something distinctive about a band of such longevity that has also managed to remain creative and vibrant. What is their secret ingredient, their Chemical X? The answer lies in Shonen Knife's potent fusion of two seemingly incongruent components: cute and cool.

Punk Rockers: Shonen Knife and Do-It-Yourself Aesthetic

Cool, or *kakkoii*, is a term usually used to describe men in Japan, while *kawaii*, or cute, to describe both girls and women (as well as babies, animals, and inanimate objects). But, as Satomi Fukutomi points out, *kakkoii* can be applied to women when they perform an activity associated with masculine behavior (Fukutomi 2010: 269). Rock, and especially punk, was (and in many ways still is) considered a white, masculine genre. The fact that the members of Shonen Knife are women, play their own instruments, and write their own songs is supremely cool by Fukutomi's standards. But while Shonen Knife embraces coolness, they never completely abandon cuteness. Naoko acknowledged that she made the most of Shonen Knife's uniqueness, telling *Rolling Stone,* "It was convenient that we are all-women band because many boy bands ask us to have a show with them" (Wild 1993). The contrasting combination of cool pop punk sounds with cute lyrics, particularly those about food, endows Shonen Knife's music with an ironic charm that delights in incongruity. The musical results are as irresistible as the delicacies they sing about. In the following pages I examine how Shonen Knife's combination of music and food complicates gender and racial stereotypes.[5]

Part of Shonen Knife's attraction has to do with the way they resist social norms; it is also what compels me to associate the band with punk culture. At first listen, few Shonen Knife songs would likely be categorized as "punk." While Shonen Knife based their sound on Ramones-style pop punk, their musical output reveals experimentation with a wide variety of genres. For example, "Boogie Monster," from the album *Heavy Songs* (2002), mingles synth pop with a 1970s disco beat. Several songs from the 1991 album *712* further illustrate Shonen Knife's diversity. The album title derives from a bit of Japanese wordplay in which numbers can be pronounced in multiple ways. In the case of "712," one could read it as "nana-ichi-futatsu," or if compressed, "na-i-fu," the Japanese transliteration for "knife." The playful approach to the album's title is apparent in its varied tracks. The opening track on *712*, "Shonen Knife," includes rap vocals accompanied by a steady drumbeat, skillfully placed repetitive bass riffs, and samples. The result is reminiscent of Tom Tom Club's "Wordy Rappinghood." "White Flag," also from *712*, references the American hardcore punk band Black Flag. The song, clocking in at just over a minute, appropriately features thrashing guitar, drums, and garbled lyrics evocative not only of Black Flag but also of the Dead Kennedy's "Nazi Punks Fuck Off."

What characterizes Shonen Knife as punk, then, is not so much their conformity to a musical genre but their origins and continued dedication as do-it-yourself (DIY) artists. In other words, in the case of Shonen Knife, the punk aesthetic is more about means than ends. In *Global Punk: Resistance and Rebellion in Everyday Life*, Kevin Dunn considers the DIY quality to be the cornerstone of punk. For him, the DIY component "involves a rejection of the passive role of the consumer. . . . [It] is a championing of personal empowerment" (Dunn 2016: 13). The decision to take action, to do something as a creative act, is what is at the heart of punk rock. Punk is as much about attitude as it is about electric rock loudness.

Shonen Knife is the epitome of DIY artists. To begin with, Naoko, Atsuko, and Michie weren't trained musicians—for the first decade of the band's career, they all maintained day jobs. When they formed the band in 1981, Naoko was working at a major machinery company as an OL (short for office lady, a phrase used to describe a female office worker), Michie at a household machinery company, and Atsuko was still a high school student. Naoko and Michie continued to work in various positions and Atsuko attended fashion school and worked as a designer until 1994's North American tour. At that point, they decided to become full-time musicians (Yamano Naoko, personal email communication, August 10, 2020). Their early recordings reveal a sparse style that some cite as lack of technical ability. What detractors fail to realize is that virtuosity is not the point of Shonen Knife's music-making. The self-taught, DIY approach to playing and songwriting is what matters. Continuing in the DIY manner, Atsuko designed most of the 1960s-style dresses the band wore in their early performance days. Shonen Knife continues working outside the mainstream idol system that has long generated the majority of Japan's pop music output. Naoko observed that this is a result of being based in Osaka instead of Tokyo, where most major music industry companies and bands reside (Yamano N., email communication, August 10, 2020). Shonen Knife established their reputation primarily through live performances on local and international indie rock circuits. The un-cute aspect of traveling in a tour bus and playing small and medium-sized venues set against happy songs about animals and ice cream underscores Shonen Knife's commitment to uniting cute with an unpretentious cool. Whether by choice or chance, Shonen Knife has never had occasion to "sell out," a charge many punk bands encounter when they achieve popular success.

In his book, Dunn also stipulates that punk is anti-status quo; it involves seeing something wrong with the world and doing something about it (Dunn 2016: 37–8). The Japanese idol system that has dominated the nation's music world for decades tends to fetishize young female performers (something agencies and production companies in Japan and the United States are equally guilty of); in action and appearance, Shonen Knife represents an alternative to the idol system. At shows, the band members are as likely to appear in T-shirts and jeans as to don fashionable Mondrian-inspired dresses. Shonen Knife does not overtly critique the mainstream popular music world, but in the very act of performing rock music on stage, they engage with the music industry and its continued objectification of young women. While the band maintains that they are not politically driven, I think it is important to recognize their role as Japanese women rock artists; in this I take the position that music, and entertainment in general, is inherently political.[6]

Naoko herself has admitted that while she writes about cute things like animals and sweets, the lyrical content often contains a double meaning and sometimes even a triple meaning (Ishihara 1993: 5). In an interview with *Girl Frenzy* magazine, she drew on food metaphors to describe this approach, relating, "the lyrics look like a chocolate peanut: the inside part of the peanut is very ironical and outside I coat the serious things with very sweet things like chocolate, so if people listen carefully they'll realise we are singing about many problems and issues" (Zara 1993: 9).[7] As Zara points out in another *Girl Frenzy* article, the early reception of Shonen Knife abroad was fraught with racist and sexist evaluations of the band. Many transcribed interviews from this time emphasized the women's accented English, describe the band members as cute and polite (a stark contrast to the Anglo-European Riot Grrrl), and comment on their lack of instrumental abilities (Zara 1993: 10). Zara critiques the music press:

> There are rarely any suggestions that Shonen Knife are taking the piss out of Americana in their refusal to play the macho tough-guy game with rock journos. . . . In the British music press, it's now fine for girls to riot and swear (and I think it's lovely when we do) but it's beyond these hacks that less macho things have a meaning in some women's lives too, LIKE Barbies and brightly-coloured sweets, and that they carry a certain weight in our personal politics. (Zara 1993: 10)

This integration of the anti-macho (cute) and the macho (cool) serves as generative source material for Shonen Knife. In their songs, the band reclaims and redeems these "less macho things" that have meaning for many listeners of all genders. Most scholarship on gender and rock concentrates on American and European artists (Kearney 2017; Bayton 1998; Reddington 2007; Leonard 2007). By more closely considering the relationship between food and gender performance in Shonen Knife's music, I hope to expand intellectual discourse on Japanese rock and roll. I first consider the history of women rock musicians in Japan. I then provide a brief explanation of the historical relationships between food, gender, and popular music in Japan. Following that, I turn my attention to an overview of Shonen Knife songs across the decades that deal with food and, by extension, gender. Next, I look specifically at the album *Happy Hour* (1998). Because *Happy Hour* marks the conclusion of Shonen Knife's early period, and because it contains so many songs about food, it is especially worthy of deeper analysis. I consider how the visual and aural elements of *Happy Hour* participate in the complex interaction between gender performance, food, and rock. I finish with a contemplation of Shonen Knife's legacy.

1 Girl Bands and *Josei* Rock, 1950s–1980s

Girls Band and/or *Josei* Rock?

Girls bands (known as *gāruzu bando* in Japanese *katakana*, the phonetic system used for foreign loanwords) have existed in some form since the beginning of rock-and-roll culture in Japan in the mid-twentieth century. There are some qualities about this denotative genre that are problematic. As the reader can surmise, *gāruzu bando* is Japanified English; the phrase itself is immediately established as foreign to the native Japanese language, and by extension to the culture itself. Additionally, the word "girl" acts as a diminutive adjective adding a patina of cuteness to the noun "band." As we will see, some, but not all, women-led groups embrace cute performance practices. The persistent use of the term "girl" demeans the grown women performing in these bands. By describing them as "girls" in the popular media, these performers' music is implicitly marginalized as commodity entertainment not to be taken seriously; it is not adult "art." Finally, the word "band" is vague as it does not indicate a musical genre. The lack of generic attachment may seem liberating, but it is in many ways a limitation. The phrase "girl bands" disassociates female-identifying performers from their musical creations. What their music sounds like seems to matter less than the fact that they are young and female.

Because of these issues, I suggest an alternative term, *josei* rock. *Josei* means "woman" or "female" in Japanese. It can be used as a general term to describe all those identifying as female. Rock, or *rokku* in Japanese, is of course a broad genre that encompasses everything from surf and new wave to hardcore and heavy metal. But the term does imply the general combination of guitar, bass, and drum set, and it references generic harmonic and melodic practices. To be sure, many of the bands I discuss in this chapter have historically been described as girl bands and some, like Princess Princess, can easily fall under the category of either pop or rock. However, I believe *josei* rock to be a more apt term that best describes the wide variety of women rock groups from Japan both in the past and in the present. Thus, for the purposes of this book, I use the phrase *josei* rock.

Josei Rock: History and Context

In this section I briefly discuss the history of rock and the dynamics of gender and race in Japan before focusing on some predecessors and contemporaries of Shonen Knife during its formative years in the 1980s. Mary Celeste Kearney explains the different ways gender politics entered into rock history in America, citing the predominance of hegemonic masculinity and a patriarchal system that came to dominate the rock scene (Kearney 2017: 55–8). Thanks to the broader political work by feminist and queer activists, rock culture in Anglo-European contexts slowly transformed in the final decades of the twentieth century (Kearney 2017: 58–60). Nevertheless, the cult of identity, and by extension gender performance, continues to influence rock today. Rock does not exist in a vacuum; as much as we might wish for a world in which all races, sexes, gender identifications, and sexual orientations receive egalitarian treatment, the world has not yet achieved this utopic ideal. Landmarks like the Rock and Roll Hall of Fame's induction of Aretha Franklin in 1987 and Sister Rosetta Tharpe in 2018 have finally highlighted the historical role of women, and especially Black women, in the genre's development in the United States. Additionally, scholarship and media are increasingly focusing attention on female artists', producers', and consumers' influences on rock culture (Kearney 2017: 123–30). Therefore, I want to highlight the contributions of some female-identifying Japanese artists who have hitherto been ignored abroad, and in some cases even in their home country.

Josei Rock Beginnings

In 1950s Japan, men and women alike were inspired by Elvis Presley and were dipping their toes into the newest popular music genre: rock and roll.[1] Among these women, Misora Hibari stands out for her long and extensive career across multiple genres: boogie-woogie, rockabilly, and most notably, *enka*, nostalgic ballads that mix Japanese traditional music elements with Western ones. While Hibari (referred to by fans and scholars alike by her given name) built her legacy on the latter genre, her activity across the board was crucial to women's participation in popular music in Japan in the second half of the twentieth century. Michael K. Bourdaghs relates that it is impossible to compare Hibari to any single Western artist, but if pressed he would describe her as "a combination of Judy Garland, Frank Sinatra, and Elvis Presley" (Bourdaghs 2012: 53). Hibari hugely influenced the world of postwar music in Japan, and generations of performers including 1960s rockers Jackie and the Blue Comets and, later, Yellow Magic Orchestra's Sakamoto Ryūichi sought collaborations with her (Bourdaghs 2012: 73). Because of Hibari's importance to Japanese popular music in the latter half of the twentieth century, a history of *josei* rock by necessity begins with Hibari and her colleagues.

Most relevant to this history is Hibari's participation in a girl group early in her career. Together with Yukimura Izumi and Eri Chiemi, the young women performed as a rockabilly group called Three Girls (*Sannin Musume*) that formed as part of a crossover promotion between Japan's film and music industries (Bourdaghs 2012: 59).[2] While most of their songs were covers of American tunes, they also sang some Japanese-language songs (albeit composed by others) (Branstetter 2019).[3] The women drew on the sound world of low registers and growls that might have been inspired by Oklahoma native Wanda Jackson and her successful tour of Japan in 1959 (Jackson with Bomar 2017: 132–3; Branstetter 2019). Misora effectively mastered the rockabilly sound in her 1958 recording "Rockabilly Swordfighting" (Rokabirī Kenpō) (Bourdaghs 2012: 66, 87; Branstetter 2019). Misora's colleague Yukimura even covered Jackson's "Fujiyama Mama," which had become a number one hit released by Capital Records' Japanese branch (Jackson with

Bomar 2017: 132–3). Yukimura transformed the Jackson tune and inserted Japanese lyrics between English ones, adopting the musical language of early rock and making it her own (Bourdaghs 2012: 87). The women of Three Girls, known for their varied musical activities in postwar Japan, are among some of the earliest female participants in rock and their influence cannot be ignored.

Just as Elvis and rockabilly swept Japan in the 1950s, Beatlemania invaded the country in the latter half of the 1960s (Bourdaghs 2012: 124–5). The rock music of this time, centered around the electric guitar, came to be known as "Group Sounds" (Bourdaghs 2012: 113–57). While young men comprised many of the era's bands, women also participated in Group Sounds, usually filling the role of vocalist.[4] Among these performers, Obata Miki stands out. She began her career as a fashion model before entering the music world in 1967 with her debut single "First Love's Letter" (Hatsukoi no retā), a tune with a surf beat featuring brass, electric guitar, and a minor-mode melody. While Obata collaborated with Nakamura Taiji on the music, she wrote the lyrics for her songs herself—an uncommon activity for female pop-music performers both then and now. In doing so, she asserted agency over her performances.

Early Beatles tunes also inspired the female band members of Pinky Chicks, originally a dance group called Sweet Roses. Leader Oka Naomi encouraged her friends to transform themselves into a rock band and capitalize on the popularity of Group Sounds. Joining Oka, the bassist and vocalist, were Itono Miwa on vocals, Hirooka Julie and Togashi Yumi on guitar, Ōtori Mika on drums, and Matsubara Miho on keyboards. With support from Japan Victor Records, the Pinky Chicks learned some tunes and performed at American military stations, small clubs, and on late-night television. They found moderate success with the ballad "Go to Your Side" (Soba ni itte) and appeared in two movies in 1968. In one of these films, *Train for the First Shrine Visit of the New Year* (*Hatsumode ressha*), the band performs a groovy tune titled "Work Song a-Go-Go" (Sōran-bushi a go-go).[5] While dancers scream and cheer, the women, dressed only in short silk robes akin to smoking jackets, dance in synchronization and perform a surf riff. "Yeah yeah yeah" comprises the majority of the lyrics. The Pinky Chicks and their 1960s attire capture the atmosphere of Group Sounds.[6] Although the Pinky Chicks were a *josei* rock group who played their own instruments, as a musical endeavor, the group was short-lived. Like many other Group Sounds bands, it dissolved in the early 1970s. Nevertheless, women shown playing rock instruments in popular media was an important step in the history of *josei* rock.

The 1970s saw the rise of women singer-songwriters in Japan just as similar artists like Joni Mitchell and Carole King were coming to prominence in the United States. Pianist-vocalists like Matsutoya Yumi and Yano Akiko debuted at this time to great acclaim and went on to influence Japanese popular music for decades. Early idol girl groups like Pink Lady and Candies also emerged around then, as the Japanese producers sought to cultivate performers and exert greater control on the industry. Concurrently, glam, electronic music, funk, soul, disco, new wave, rock, and punk were also flowing into Japan's popular music ether. And toward the end of the 1970s and the beginning of the 1980s, a large number of female musical groups appeared on the scene, representing the first wave of *josei* rock. Shonen Knife were active participants in this first wave, but so were many other groups that were not able to sustain their careers beyond the 1980s. In the remainder of this chapter, I discuss some of these *josei* rock bands. These women made important contributions to the world of Japanese rock that have gone unheeded in both Japanese and English-language scholarship to date.

Josei Rock's First Wave

A few qualities differentiate the artists of *josei* rock's first wave from their predecessors. First, many of the musicians in the first wave of *josei* rock wrote and recorded their own songs and played rock instruments. While control over their music and image depended on their relationship with the music industry, the fact that women were not relegated to the role of vocalist is important. Second, as mentioned earlier, idol culture also appeared around this time. The women rockers sometimes starkly contrasted with idols' squeaky-clean images and concomitant squeaky, high-pitched voices. At other times, female rock musicians borrowed and capitalized on idol culture in potent ways. Importantly, though, many groups exercised some agency over how gender performance would come into play musically and on stage. Third, the first wave of *josei* rock arose at a time when women rockers in other parts of the world were also attracting attention. Fanny, Exene Cervenka, Patti Smith, Chrissie Hynde, Siouxsie Sioux, Poly Styrene, Debbie Harry, the Slits, Heart, the Runaways, and the Go-Go's all appeared on the scene in the 1970s and early

1980s. Shonen Knife and the groups described below were participating, consciously or not, in a global movement by women rockers challenging the genre's patriarchal elements.[7]

Finally, Japan's economic conditions also influenced the course of *josei* rock. Around this time, Japan's economy had achieved phenomenal growth. By the 1970s and 1980s, Japanese electronics and cars were dominating the global economy, and until 2010, Japan's GDP was second only to that of the United States. The country's growing economic clout affected women and the feminist movement, including education and employment. The percentage of women attending junior and four-year colleges had septupled between 1955 and 1981 (Fujimura-Fanselow 1985: 475). About 50 percent of women worked outside the home, though many had to choose between pursuing a lifelong career comparable to men's and undertaking part-time work while also performing the duties expected of a housewife (Kano 2016: 18–19, 125, 149). Ayako Kano describes, "The *feminizumu* [feminism] boom in the 1980s was at once commercial, political, and academic in nature, as the era of women (*onna no jidai*) became a slogan for marketers as well as for activists and scholars" (Kano 2016: 18–19). *Josei* rock participated in the decade's *feminizumu* boom, both directly and indirectly. By taking this historical context into consideration, we can better appreciate the musical, cultural, and even political work of Shonen Knife and their contemporaries in a global context.

One early example of the exchange between Japanese rockers and those across the Pacific is GIRLS' cover of the Runaways' "Cherry Bomb." Founded in 1977, GIRLS was together for only two years, and the majority of their tracks are disco influenced and less heavy than the Runaways' tune. In their cover of "Cherry Bomb," released as the B-side on their debut album *Nora Neko* (*Stray Cat*), lead singer Rita (Nomoto Takako) alternates between Japanese-language verses and an English-language chorus. The easy switching between the two languages is a significant gesture that remains a staple for much of rock music in Japan. GIRLS' version of "Cherry Bomb" follows the original closely, albeit without the orgasmic moans.[8] GIRLS went on to record other covers, such as Blondie's "In the Flesh" and a disco version of the Ramones'"Sheena Is a Punk Rocker." As early *josei* rockers, they unabashedly embraced the commodification of both their musical abilities and their sex appeal; the album cover for *Nora Neko* shows the women posing sassily and leader Rita stands with her legs splayed, wearing hot pants and a leopard print corset.

In their overt sexuality, GIRLS' image contrasts with their close contemporaries, Mizutama Shōbōdan (Polka Dot Fire Brigade). Formed in 1979, the group billed itself as "five women who make their own songs and play guitars, keyboard, bass, and drums."[9] Mizutama Shōbōdan's sound is difficult to describe. They are experimental rock, and their lead singer Tenko rarely intones a lyrical melody. Instead, much of her singing is akin to *Sprechsgesang*, or a sing-speaking style in the vein of the B52's male vocalist Fred Schneider. However, Mizutama Shōbōdan's music is much noisier than this popular American new wave band. They eschewed standard song structures, hooks, and clearly delineated harmonic progressions; in this way, Mizutama Shōbōdan introduced elements of an international avant-gardism into *josei* rock. Early on in the band's career, Tenko established her own record label called *Kinniku Bijo* (Muscled

Beauty) and released the band's two albums, *The Virgin's Prayers Are Da! Da! Da!* (*Otome no inori wa da da da*) (1981) and *Sky Full of Red Petals* (*Manten ni akai hanabira*) (1985). Mizutama Shōbōdan exercised artistic as well as commercial control over their work. Their strident rejection of the mainstream allowed them to create music without considering the pressures of selling records and packing venues. Yet this approach also limited circulation and awareness of Mizutama Shōbōdan's music.

Conversely, two important bands of the 1980s had little trouble cultivating broad appeal. Show-ya and Princess Princess were hugely successful rock groups that capitalized on femininity. Show-ya embraced sexiness, while Princess Princess promoted cuteness. Both bands typically had very little control over their music. Nevertheless, the visibility of these *josei* rock groups in Japanese mass media was crucial to the bands of later generations. Show-ya, a five-piece heavy metal band, formed in 1981. Vocalist Terada Keiko and keyboardist and leader Nakamura Miki formed the core of the group. Joining them were Tsunoda Miki on drums, Igarashi Miki on guitar, and Senba Satomi on bass. The band's name is a play on both English and Japanese. In English "show ya" conveys a sense of challenge, in the vein of "I'll show you!" It also subtly hints at sexual awakening, as in "I'll show you mine if you show me yours." "Show ya" also is a pun on the Shōwa emperor, whose long reign (1926–1989) encompassed the Second World War, the American Occupation from 1945 to 1952, and the rise of Japan as a global economic power. Again, the wordplay between English and Japanese helps establish this quality as a trope common in *josei* rock.

The band received attention from music executives when it won the ladies' division of a Yamaha-sponsored battle of the bands in 1982.[10] Terada was offered a solo contract but turned it down to remain with the band. During their early years, the women wrote most of their own music; their second album, *Queendom* (1986), features songs solely by the band members, with Terada providing most of the lyrics. Show-ya's taste of success led them to seek out more mainstream audiences, and by 1987 they were collaborating with the idol system svengali Akimoto Yasushi, founder of Onyanko Club and AKB48.[11] The result was that Show-ya gained national attention but ceded their creative agency. They no longer wrote most of their music and lyrics, and Terada's image became even more sexualized. But the success of becoming a national act allowed Show-ya to contribute to the establishment of important institutions supporting *josei* rock. Just as Tenko founded her own record label in 1987, Show-ya established *Naon no yaon* (Women's Outdoor Concert Hall), an all-Japanese, all-female music festival that continued to be held on a regular basis until 1999. Success also eventually allowed Show-ya to regain some independence: the 1989 album *Outerlimits*, featuring music and lyrics primarily by the band, made it to number three on the Japan Oricon charts.

The single "Limited Lovers" (Genkai Lovers) from *Outerlimits* represents Show-ya at their best. It opens with an aggressive, upper-register guitar riff. Non-stop drums soon join in. The bass thumps out driving eighth notes, and the keyboard punctuates formal changes at the verse's B section and chorus. Terada sings in a husky middle range that cuts through the dense instrumentation and her voice evokes Bruce Dickinson, the singer for Iron Maiden. Igarashi shreds the guitar solo; by the end of the song, there is no doubt the women of Show-ya know how to rock. The year after *Outerlimits* came out, in 1990, the band played at the massive Budōkan arena in Tokyo, a pinnacle of musical achievement. But Show-ya was not the first all-female rock group to play at the Budōkan. Shortly prior, their contemporaries Princess Princess played there.

Among the bands discussed in this section, Princess Princess achieved the highest level of popularity. This success was partly because the band was originally conceived as an idol group; the members did not know each other beforehand. Instead, TDK Records held auditions in 1983 for young women who hoped to join the label's new, all-female band. The women selected—Okui Kaori, Nakayama Kanako, Watanabe Atsuko, Kono Tomoko, and Tomita Kyoko—worked to master their instruments and performance practices after the fact.[12] In 1987, they released their first single, "Love Is Balance" (Koi wa baransu), which later appeared on the 1987 album *Teleportation*. Nakayama provided the lyrics, but producer Suzuki Saburō wrote the music. At first, the band struggled to find a niche in the popular market, but then the women decided that they would write both music and lyrics themselves. Significantly, they also employed a female manager, Ichimura Emiko. Princess Princess continued playing small venues and finally received critical acclaim with their 1988 album *Here We Are*.

A mixture of rock and pop, Princess Princess soon became immensely successful, selling out tickets to a show at Shibuya Public Hall in Tokyo in less than two hours in 1988, and going on to sell out the Nippon Budōkan in 1989. The Budōkan is a special monument to modern Japan and to rock and roll. The martial arts hall was constructed for the 1964 Tokyo Olympics. These Olympics were a milestone in postwar Japan; they signified Japan's miraculous recovery from wartime devastation and ushered the country into the global community (Rhoads and McCorkle 2018: 71–3). A couple of years later, in 1966, the Beatles performed there. Since then, numerous artists from both Japan and overseas played at the Budōkan, but Princess Princess was the first all-female Japanese rock group to perform in the hallowed space.[13] The same year as their Budōkan concert, Princess Princess solidified their stardom with their 1989 number one single "Diamonds."

"Diamonds" is a verse-pre-chorus-chorus song in a major key, with Okui's vocals about love and nostalgia cutting clearly through the instrumental accompaniment. The snare is prominent in the mix, with the synthesizer and bass in the background. The guitar is almost inaudible until the instrumental bridge and outro. Because the mix of the song de-emphasizes electric guitar in favor of synthesizer and high-pitched vocals, the song sounds more musically aligned with late 1980s idol pop than with rock. In various recordings of live performances available on YouTube, Okui shuffles her feet in time with the music, a dance move similar to those of singing idols. All in all, compared to Show-ya, with whom Princess Princess sometimes shared a bill, "Diamonds" is spritely and cute. This is the kind of rock that Japanese parents could feel comfortable about their little girls enjoying. Despite their softer image, Princess Princess paved the way for female rock musicians in Japan in the 1980s and the 1990s. They reclaimed agency over their musical material, employed women in management, and were highly visible in the media, all of which influenced the future of *josei* rock.

If GIRLS and Mizutama Shōbōdan represent the indie realm of the *josei* rock world and Show-ya and Princess Princess the mainstream one, where does Shonen Knife fit in? Shonen Knife's music features elements as creative as those of Mizutama, as hardcore as Show-ya and GIRLS, and sometimes as poppy as Princess Princess. As explored in the following chapters, despite frequently being labelled a pop punk, Shonen Knife's music varies widely. Instead of narrowing themselves into an easily marketed niche, the band draws from a wide swathe of Japan's musical past and present. They successfully blend incongruous elements together, often with delicious results.

2 Food, Gender, and Music in Postwar Japan

Shonen Knife's lineup evolved over the decades, with Naoko anchoring the group and writing the majority of songs.[1] Shonen Knife's sound also developed, shifting from a new wave punk vibe in the early 1980s to a heavier glam rock texture present in albums like *Overdrive* (2014) and *Adventure* (2016). But one thing remains constant in Shonen Knife's music: their continued devotion to songs about food. Shonen Knife are hardly the only Japanese musicians to sing about food, but they are exceptional in the sheer number of food songs that they have consistently released throughout their career.[2] While some artists may write one or two songs about food over the course of their career, Shonen Knife repeatedly returns to the topic. From "I Wanna Eat Chocobars" (*Pretty Little Baka Guy*, 1986) to "Ramen Rock" (*Overdrive,* 2014), and "Green Tangerine" (*Adventure,* 2016), almost every Shonen Knife album contains at least one song about food. Even their nineteenth studio album, *Sweet Candy Power* (2019), includes two food-inspired tracks.

To date, I have identified at least forty Shonen Knife songs that are related to food as outlined in Table 2.1.[3] The band members clearly love food and this fascination helps connect them with their fan base. The band's 1998 book *Shonen Knife*

Table 2.1 *Timeline of Shonen Knife's Songs about Food*

Track	Album	Year
"Cannibal Papaya"	*Everyone Have Fun; Yama No Attchan*	1982; 1984
"Flying Jelly Attack"	*Yama No Attchan; Let's Knife*	1984; 1992
"I Wanna Eat Chocobars"	*Pretty Little Baka Guy*	1986
"Ice Cream City"	*Pretty Little Baka Guy*	1986
"Fruit Loop Dream"	*712*	1991
"Blue Oyster Cult"	*712*	1991
"Diet Run"	*712*	1991
"Tomato Head"	*Rock Animals*	1993
"Brown Mushrooms"	*Rock Animals*	1993
"Strawberry Cream Puff"	*Rock Animals*	1993
"Wonder Wine"	*Brand New Knife*	1997
"Fruits & Vegetables"	*Brand New Knife*	1997
"Hot Chocolate"	*It's a New Find; Happy Hour*	1997; 1998
"Cookie Day"	*Happy Hour*	1998
"Gyoza"	*Happy Hour*	1998
"Banana Chips"	*Happy Hour*	1998
"Sushi Bar Song"	*Happy Hour*	1998
"Sesame"	*Strawberry Sound*	2000
"Mayonnaise Addiction"	*Strawberry Sound*	2000
"Herbs"	*Orange Sun*	2001

Table 2.1 (Continued)

Track	Album	Year
"Mango Juice"	*Heavy Songs*	2002
"Heavy Song"	*Heavy Songs*	2002
"Monkey Brand Oolong Tea"	*Candy Rock*	2003
"Broccoli Man"	*Genki Shock!*	2006
"Popcorn"	*Fun! Fun! Fun!*	2007
"I Wanna Eat Cookies"	*Fun! Fun! Fun!*	2007
"Deer Biscuits"	*Super Group*	2008
"BBQ Party"	*Super Group*	2008
"Rock 'n' Roll Cake"	*Free Time*	2010
"P.Y.O."	*Free Time*	2010
"Sweet Christmas"	*Sweet Christmas*	2011
"All You Can Eat"	*Pop Tune*	2012
"Ramen Rock"	*Overdrive*	2014
"Fortune Cookie"	*Overdrive*	2014
"Green Tea"	*Overdrive*	2014
"Wasabi"	*Adventure*	2016
"Cotton Candy Clouds"	*Adventure*	2016
"Green Tangerine"	*Adventure*	2016
"Ice Cream Cookie Sandwiches"	*Sweet Candy Power*	2019
"Sweet Candy Power"	*Sweet Candy Power*	2019

Land includes artwork, interviews, and the band members' favorite recipes: *takoyaki* (fried dough balls with octopus inside), *okonomiyaki* (a savory Japanese pancake), salmon sandwich, and *sōmen* noodle salad. It also features "Naoko's Food Comparison Report," in which she describes eating fried beef cutlets with Nirvana and trying matzo ball soup for the first time in Los Angeles, as well as other foodie escapades. On their 2017 Ramen Adventure Tour, Shonen Knife regularly visited ramen restaurants at tour stops, posting pictures of each shop on social media. Food is as much a part of their artistic output as it is their everyday lives. Why are the members of Shonen Knife so concerned with food and what are we listeners to make of this borderline obsession? Does food have some symbolic importance in Shonen Knife's oeuvre? In this chapter, I delve into the significance of food in Japanese culture and consider its role in Japanese popular music traditions prior to the formation of Shonen Knife. Doing so can help us better understand why food is central to Shonen Knife.

The field of food studies may hold some answers to the above questions. In their detailed examination of food in Japanese culture, social anthropologists Michael Ashkenazi and Jeanne Jacob discuss food's importance in relation to philosophy, religion, history, and everyday life. Of particular note is their discussion on food and gender. They describe certain foods like meat as typically associated with masculinity, and sweets with femininity (Ashkenazi and Jacob 2000: 105). However, the authors acknowledge that the actual world of food consumption in Japan is not so neatly binary: "At the time of eating that food, it might be a statement of a particular gender position. But, the Japanese are ready to concede, perhaps it is not. Ambiguity and indirection, playfulness rather than seriousness, is the name of the game" (Ashkenazi and Jacob 2000: 110). Thus, food consumption can be, but is not necessarily always, an element of gender performance (Butler 1990; 2006). The nebulous nature of eating opens up a space for play where multiple meanings can exist simultaneously. Through their music about food, Shonen Knife enacts a fluid social position that demonstrates different ways of performing gender. Food is food, but, whether we are conscious of it or not, it is rarely *just* food. The same can be said of music, and in Shonen Knife, music and food, two key components of culture, come together.

Food, like music, also has the potential to facilitate relationships between people. We all recognize this connection; in many cultures around the world, food is a means of showing welcome to neighbors or affection for loved ones. This is equally true in Japan. Anne Allison (2000) and more recently Ayako Kano (2016) have noted the way mothers translate their love into carefully crafted lunchboxes for their preschool-aged children. Kano points out

> excessively decorated lunches, especially those featuring the images of superheroes and cute characters from anime and TV shows—painstakingly constituted through slices of ham, slivers of seaweed, spikes of uncooked spaghetti concealed for internal support—have become popular, perhaps even normative, by being featured in publications targeted to children as well as those targeting mothers. (2016:104–5)

Women are considered the primary providers of food to family members in the domestic sphere while male master chefs dominate Japan's haute cuisine. Women's cooking, while equally labor intensive in terms of gustatory and visual components, is about relationships and family. Yet in recent years in Japanese literary culture, some authors have complicated the connection between food preparations and gender roles. Tomoko Aoyama outlines that in post-industrial Japan, as reflected for instance in works like Yoshimoto Banana's *Kitchen* (*Kitchin*) (1988) and Tawara Machi's *Salad Anniversary* (*Sarada kinenbi*) (1987), "food inspires and unites people" (Aoyama 1999: 113–14). The works, especially Yoshimoto's, portray interpersonal relationships, food, and its consumption as gender-fluid. The specific role of gendered food preparation is relevant to understanding Shonen Knife's music.

Musicologists writing about popular music have observed the ways music is a vehicle for gender performance. While several have investigated the role of gender and sexuality in the rock world, Susan McClary's evaluation of Madonna is an especially relevant text (McClary 1991: 148–66). In her analysis of Madonna as a popular female musician, McClary discusses the misogynistic history of Western music in the classical and popular spheres. She writes, "The barriers that have prevented them [women] from participation have occasionally been formal: in the seventeenth century there were even papal edicts proscribing women's musical education. More often, however, women are discouraged through more subtle means from considering themselves as potential musicians" (McClary 1991: 150). These "subtle means" include lack of support, accessibility, and general discouragement from authority figures. The original members of Shonen Knife faced similar obstacles. In an interview with MTV in 1991, Michie related, "My parents totally hated me playing music." Naoko added, "My mother said, 'Don't walk around my house with your guitar, because neighbors [will] look and say she's crazy'" (*MTV News* 1991).

In an observation that is not limited to female-identifying performers, McClary points out that most performers rely on sexual appeal: "Women on the performance stage are viewed as sexual commodities regardless of their appearance or seriousness" (McClary 1991: 151). This kind of assessment is sometimes true of Shonen Knife. A discomforting tone occasionally emerges on online message boards concerning their appearance, their bodies, and male sexual desires even though the band shuns overt sexuality in their music and performance (they have almost no songs about love and typically wear attractive, modest attire in concert and promotional photographs). Instead of expressing romantic and by extension sexual desire, many of the songs by Shonen Knife express a different kind of desire: one for food.[4] Food is a polysemic topic that allows the band and its listeners to play with the multiple ways music and text can be interpreted.

Kinda Cute, Kinda Cool, Kinda Wild

What do the prolific references to food in Shonen Knife's songs tell us about cuteness and gender in Japan at the turn of the millennium? Anthropologist Christine Yano's work on Hello Kitty sheds light on this question. In the opening pages of her book *Pink Globalization: Hello Kitty's Trek Across the Pacific*, Yano describes a photograph of young women dressed in ultra-cute garb in numerous shades of pink, along with Hello Kitty accoutrements (2013: 2–3). She argues that "In the insouciant style of these Tokyo women, the look is not sweet but highly ironic, no-holds-barred cute. It is in-your-face cute as a highly stylized, overwrought visual aesthetic." Yano continues, suggesting that "Japanese Cute-Cool, as exemplified by Hello Kitty, inhabits a commodified space of pink global visibility" (2013: 5). While Shonen Knife's music is not as omnipresent as Hello Kitty, their musical output also resides in this "commodified space of pink global visibility." I find some connections between the overwhelming forces of Hello Kitty's cuteness, as adopted by many people of all gender identifications around the world, and the music and image of Shonen Knife. The band, like the young women bedecked in Hello Kitty garb, embraces an unapologetic, tongue-in-cheek cute-cool.

This link between Shonen Knife, Hello Kitty, and rebelliousness is not so far-flung; some fans consider Hello Kitty to represent, in her assertive cuteness, a punk vibe (2013: 199). The Riot Grrrl movement, a feminist punk network prominent on the west coast of the United States in the 1990s and 2000s, famously embraced "girly" culture, like Hello Kitty (2013: 202). A reclamation of cuteness, whether ironic or sincere, reflected one of the movement's goals to reinvent punk culture as both feminine and feminist (2013: 202). As Yano describes, "Sporting Kitty, then, becomes a way for these punk women to thumb their nose at stereotypes, saying, in effect, 'We can appropriate cute for our own purposes, on our own terms'" (2013: 202).

The food-based lyrics are a source of Shonen Knife's defiant cuteness. Like Hello Kitty and other cute products, the band's music is a "happy object." Sarah Ahmed explains how a happy object functions: "Groups cohere around a shared orientation toward some things as being good, treating some things and not others as the cause of delight. If the same objects make us happy . . . then we would be oriented or directed in the same way" (Ahmed 2010: 35; cited in Yano 2013: 20). Shonen Knife orients much of their music around the ultimate happy object: food. By concentrating so much of their lyrical output on cookies, cake, and other delicious dishes, Shonen Knife invokes a pan-cultural "happy object."

Beyond the lyrics, the musical components frequently function as aural happy objects. The vast majority of Shonen Knife's songs are in a happy-sounding major key at an upbeat tempo with the requisite drums, guitar, and bass. Songs tend to be in a familiar verse-chorus or verse-bridge structure with an instrumental interlude (similar to many Ramones songs), but also often feature extended formats and key modulations. As a collective result, even Shonen Knife songs about food poisoning ("Blue Oyster Cult," *712* [1991]) and man-eating fruit ("Cannibal Papaya," *Everyone Have Fun, Yama No Attchan* [1982; 1984]) can sound cheerful.

Japanese Food Culture

In addition to the gendered component of food, it is, like music, extremely important to defining culture. This is as true in Japan as it is elsewhere around the world. With a food culture that is hundreds of years old, Japan continues to treat food as a cornerstone of its national cultural identity. In 2013, UNESCO recognized *washoku,* traditional Japanese cuisine, as Intangible Cultural Heritage (Rath 2016). In contemporary Japan, it is impossible to turn on the television without encountering some show about food, whether it is an instructive show on how to prepare delicious dinners, comedians trying the latest Tokyo food fad, or a news host visiting a rural restaurant specializing in a local delicacy. Japanese media seems obsessed with food, in part because it is such a crucial part to maintaining national cultural identity in a world that is becoming increasingly international. Scholars like Emiko Ohnuki-Tierney explored food's significance to Japan. She is quick to recognize the fluidity of food as a symbol, and in her analysis rice represents an ideal metaphor for Japanese identity (Ohnuki-Tierney 1993: 4). Rice planting and harvesting was an important part of the agricultural season, when communities would come together to complete the tasks in a timely matter (Ohnuki-Tierney 1993: 5). Historically, rice was considered a sign of affluence that only wealthy elite could afford to eat on a regular basis. It thus became a symbol of social standing early on, a dish to be cherished and honored. Even today, rice and rice-based dishes like *mochi* (glutinous rice ball) are an important part of New Year's good luck rituals; families frequently place bottles of sake, an alcohol made from fermented rice, on shrines to honor ancestors, and a schoolchild will be roundly scolded for not eating all of their rice at lunch. Rice, whether it is a large or small portion, is considered by many to be an essential component of a meal. It is no wonder that the Japanese word for cooked rice, *gohan*, is synonymous with "meal."

Ishige Naomichi's entry on Japanese food and drink in *The Cambridge World History of Food* similarly emphasizes Japan's unique rice and fish-based diet and relationship in a way that belies a culinary nationalism (Ishige 2000: 1175–82). In the conclusion to his entry, Ishige opines that the Japanese diet was "modernized" by the lifting of taboos on beef in the late nineteenth century and the proliferation of bread and foreign sweets in the twentieth century. He writes:

> The Japanese intake of chief nutrients reached an almost ideal level by the end of the 1970s, except for a little too much salt and a lack of calcium. The general physique has improved accordingly and the average lifespan has become the longest in the world. This ideal situation, however, may not continue long, as the generation now being raised in this affluent society on a high-protein diet may later pat a stiff price in geriatric diseases as a result of overnutrition—a problem that is becoming acute in other developed nations. (Ishige 2000: 1182)

Ishige's warning about high-protein (i.e., Western) diets potentially harming the "Japanese" body may seem trivial, but in fact the fear of foreign cultural infiltration is a potent tool for those seeking to protect traditional cuisine. Although merely a mundane warning about eating too much meat, exhortations like Ishige's can easily become a tool of nationalist rhetoric; similar moral advice about food was part of Japanese military propaganda in the 1930s and 1940s (Rath 2015: 148–9). For some scholars and politicians, both past and present, fast food and cookies pose as much a threat to the preservation of Japanese culture as punk rock.

Ishige, though, fails to acknowledge that Japanese cuisine has heavily influenced other countries' food practices; culinary exchange and influence flow in multiple directions (Albala 2018: 35–6). Additionally, as Katarzyna Cwiertka has documented, "Multiculturalism is the defining feature of the culinary scene in contemporary Japan" (Cwiertka 2006: 7). For example, everything from upscale ramen joints, fresh-from-the-sea sushi bars, Korean *yakiniku* places, fancy Chinese restaurants, Indian curry stands, American fast food chains, and ubiquitous bakeries and French patisseries line Tokyo's streets. Additionally, there are many dishes that are hybrids of these national cuisines—flaky curry bread, sweet red bean and butter baguettes, and *man* (Chinese steamed buns) filled with pizza toppings are all common. Similar to Japan's diverse food scene, a variety of genres make up the music world of contemporary Japan: jazz (Atkins 2001), hip-hop (Condry 2006; Manabe 2006), hardcore (Matsue 2009), noise music (Novak 2013), reggae (Sterling 2010), pop (Bourdaghs 2012), classical (Galliano 2002), and rock (Cope 2007). These "foreign" genres are as much a part of contemporary Japan's musical ecosystem as the so-called traditional sounds of *enka* songs, *taiko* drumming, and *gagaku*, or court music. Both food and music are transnational commodities that circulate across cultures and are transformed by these exchanges. Clinging desperately to notions of authenticity, whether in regard to food or to music, is a conceited fantasy.[5]

Food and Music in Japan: A Prehistory

Food culture is inescapable in Japanese popular culture, including music, and Shonen Knife builds on a history of food songs in Japanese popular music. The following songs show

how Japanese musicians of the past incorporated food into their own works. Many of the tunes discussed in this section feature Western-style instruments, though their melodies and harmonies are rooted in the pentatonic scales of traditional Japanese music. This combination of Japanese and Western musical styles is called *kayōkyoku* and was a popular music genre in the years prior to the Second World War. In the immediate postwar era and especially during the American Occupation (1945–52), the genre saw a resurgence.

Historian John Dower has documented the scarcity of food in Japan during the wartime and postwar eras (1999). The shortage shaped popular culture, including music. In his book *Sayonara Amerika, Sayonara Nippon,* Michael K. Bourdaghs discusses music in the postwar era in detail and singles out one food-related song for its significance: "The Apple Song" (Ringo no uta) (2012: 12). Featured in the 1945 film *Gentle Breeze* (*Soyokaze*), the movie and song were made during the wartime era but had to be adjusted following Japan's surrender in August of that year. The story focuses on a young woman named Michi (played by Namiki Michiko) who dreams of becoming a singer. At one point in the film, she wanders through an orchard, enjoying a fresh apple with children and greeting farmers. With lyrics by Satō Hachirō and music by film producer Manjome Tadashi, the tune represents not only a return to this prewar *kayōkyoku* genre but also a return to optimism in popular songs. Throughout the war, *gunka*, or military songs, dominated the airwaves, so "The Apple Song" was a welcome change. Strings, woodwinds, and brass accompany Namiki as she skips through the orchard and an idyllic village, singing a gentle meditation on consuming a red apple under the blue skies. The chorus repeats the line "The apple is lovely, lovely is the apple" (*ringo kawaii ya kawaii ya ringo*). In the immediate postwar era, starvation remained a huge problem, and the idea of eating a lovely apple was a luxurious dream for many.[6] This song played an important role in shaping postwar music culture in that it gave many, especially those in urban areas, a sense of hope, all in the form of a simple apple. When Nippon Columbia released the recording in early 1946, it sold over 100,000 copies. The success made "The Apple Song" one of the first postwar Japanese hits. It also established a crucial connection between food and happiness in Japanese popular music, a connection maintained and strengthened by Shonen Knife.

"Minnesota Egg Seller" (Minnesota no tamago uri) from 1951 was another popular *kayōkyoku*. Written by Saeki Takao (lyrics) and Tone Ichirō (music), the actress-singer Akatsuki Teruko performed the tune. Akatsuki was known for her boogie-woogie tunes that were popular at the time, and "Minnesota Egg Seller" contains some elements of that American-influenced genre. The song is in a minor mode with piano, brass, woodwinds, strings, and woodblock. Akatsuki's voice cuts through with a belting power characteristic of female boogie-woogie singers. The opening vocalizations mimic the chicken's cluck—"ko ko ko ko ko ke ko"—and are repeated as if a solitary call-and-response. The "clucks" also call to mind the cries of street vendors, some of whom you can still hear in Japan today (the baked sweet potato vendor has a particularly distinctive song). In "Minnesota Egg Seller," Atsuki relates that her product is in high demand. In the second and third verses, it is revealed that she is the best singer and the most beautiful woman in town, thanks to eating eggs.

The song's lyrics might seem odd to Americans as Minnesota is not particularly known for its eggs. It is possible that the use of Minnesota in the song lyrics was simply one of convenience; the state name is four syllables, each ending with a vowel sound that suits the Japanese language nicely. Beyond that, even though Minnesota has little to do with egg production and exportation, the "land of 10,000 lakes" existed as a pristine rural locale in the imagination of 1950s Japanese. It is also crucial that this American countryside is associated with the egg, a staple of Japanese diets by this point and a cheap source of protein during a time when meat was a pricey commodity. What is fascinating, then, about "Minnesota Egg Seller" is that America is linked with a simple food that is consumed around the globe, but not only that: the Minnesota eggs are clearly superior to all other eggs in terms of their health benefits (according to the song lyrics, that is). In this way, "Minnesota Egg Seller" is an early example of a Japanese popular song that links a foreign country, in this case the United States, to food.

Audiences in the United States made a similar connection between Japan and food, albeit in a roundabout manner. The first Japanese artist to have a major international hit was *kayōkyoku* crooner Sakamoto Kyū. Sakamoto first made a name for himself as a rockabilly singer covering Elvis Presley songs in Japanese (Bourdaghs 2012: 97). Bourdaghs describes Sakamoto's early 1961 cover of Presley's "G.I. Blues." Sakamoto, in his Japanese-language version of the song, adapted the tune to convey agency to the people of Occupied Japan and their concerns (2012: 98–101). Yet it was Sakamoto's late 1961 song "I Look Upward as I Walk" (Ue o muite arukō) that achieved success in the United States (2012: 102). Written by Ei Rokusuke with music by Nakamura Hachidai, the singing protagonist looks upward in order to keep his disappointed tears from falling. Xylophone, strings, brass, and drum set accompany Sakamoto's tuneful voice. "I Look Upward as I Walk" is in a verse-bridge structure with a whistled solo. Harmonically, both the verse and bridge constantly shift between major and minor chords (G major and E minor in the verse, C major and C minor in the bridge); this gives the song a bittersweet flavor that teeters between joy and despair. The tune went on to sell over thirteen million copies worldwide and has since been covered by many artists in Japan and beyond. It also was the first Japanese song to chart on *Billboard Hot 100*. The catch: record executives changed the song's title to "Sukiyaki" (2012: 102–3). Sukiyaki is a popular Japanese meat dish that servicemen commonly ate when stationed in Japan during the Occupation and the Korean War. Released as a single in the United States in 1963, the new title was meant to appeal to Americans who had no reference to Japanese culture aside from the delicious beef dish (2012: 106). American record companies observed that food could provide an accessible entryway to market other cultural products, like popular music.

In the postwar era, food and music were linked together in both the Japanese and American popular imaginations. In devoting a sizable amount of their musical oeuvre to songs about food, Shonen Knife maintains this connection. But for Shonen Knife, a *josei* rock band in the early 1980s, food also becomes a multivalent symbol that can simultaneously reference shifting local and global cultural dynamics, identities, and gender roles. Like Japan's modern culinary world, Shonen Knife's music, especially their songs about food, belies a rich diversity of influences, fusions, and flavors.

3 Shonen Knife's Songs in the Key of Food

A Typology of Food Songs

Shonen Knife helped solidify the alliance between food and J-pop in the global imagination. Many of their songs deal with various aspects of food and consumption though most concentrate on the pleasures of eating. This chapter discusses a few songs that are representative of some general categories of songs. Although these categories are porous, they provide one way of understanding the importance of food in Shonen Knife's songs.

Body Image and Song

Songs about food and body image are the least numerous in Shonen Knife's output; the only tunes directly dealing with this topic are "Diet Run" (*712*, 1991) and "Heavy Song" (*Heavy Songs*, 2002).[1] Both are anomalies in that they express anxiety rather than joyful abandon about food, but as such, they reflect an important aspect of relationships with food that are frequently associated with women. Food-related complexes and body negativity are in no way limited to women, but in both Western and Japanese popular cultures, the diet industry has historically targeted female consumers, capitalizing on insecurities made acute by mass media. This is why "Diet Run" and "Heavy Song" are important in Shonen Knife's work. While the band does not focus on the fraught relationship many women have with food, they do acknowledge it, and via this acknowledgment, interrogate and transform these anxieties.

The band's first hit single, "Twist Barbie" (*Burning Farm*, 1983), subtly hints at body image issues that become more apparent in the later tunes. Although "Twist Barbie" does not deal with food per se, I do not think it is possible to reference Barbie without conjuring the body image baggage associated with the impossibly shaped, blonde-haired, blue-eyed doll. The "Barbie effect" and its negative impact on young girls trying to live up to the impossible physical "ideals" of the doll's proportions has been extensively documented (Dittmar, Halliwell, and Ive 2006: 283–92). While Barbie has not always been a success in Japan, she is inextricably linked to American culture (Pollack 1996). In Japan, Barbie is an exotic Other, unlike the more popular girls' doll Licca. So why did Shonen Knife write a song about Barbie? Author Denise Sullivan calls the song "a backward anthem—not exactly a rant—about what girls who buy into the beauty myth are forced to deal with from the earliest age: the pressure to look like something they're not" (Sullivan 2001: 69). Naoko has said she preferred Barbie over Licca as a child, and reflected on this. In an interview she related

> When I was a child I had some Barbie dolls and when I wrote "Twist Barbie" I was reminded about Barbie dolls. I thought I

wanted to be like Barbie because she has a very skinny body and looks very sexy but actually I don't want to be a Barbie doll because she is made of plastic, and I don't want to be like plastic (laughs). (Zara 1993: 9)

Given Naoko's comments, I believe "Twist Barbie" represents an engagement with issues like body image, a theme that haunts later songs like "Diet Run" and "Heavy Song."

"Twist Barbie" also encompasses many of the stylistic qualities that go on to define Shonen Knife. In Shonen Knife's early years, most songs were in Japanese, but "Twist Barbie" is primarily in English with some Japanese sprinkled in at the end. In this, the song is a bellwether for the future of Shonen Knife's lyrics, in which English became the predominant language. The song itself sounds simultaneously familiar and fresh. The quirky introduction, with its punctuated guitar line and drums accenting offbeats, endows the tune with a tinge of punk new wave with a splash of surf-rock fun. The 1960s feel of the chorus is complemented by its chant of "Bang, bang, bang, twist Barbie," which references Chubby Checker's 1960 cover of "The Twist" (originally by Hank Ballard and the Midnighters) and the Beatles' 1963 cover of "Twist and Shout" (*Please Please Me*).

The Beatles' influence on Shonen Knife is evident throughout their output. While Shonen Knife is often compared to the Ramones, their musical creativity and eclecticism is more akin to that of the lads from Liverpool than the boys from Queens. Naoko described the band's variety of influences as including "'60s pops, psychedelic music, before and after '80s punk, Southeast Asian pops, reggae, Motown sounds, rock and roll, and more" (Sullivan 2001: 66). Here in "Twist Barbie," the stacked, ascending vocal harmonies and the "ooo, ahhhs" are reminiscent of 1960s girl groups like the Shirelles and the Beatles' "Twist and Shout." And just as the Beatles' performance of that song on Ed Sullivan ushered in a new era of rock and roll, so too does Shonen Knife's "Twist Barbie" crack open a musical space that is simultaneously retro and radical.

First, as explored in Chapter 1, in early 1980s Japan, a group of three women playing a rock venue was still very much an exception to the rule; moreover, these women were not playing into stereotypical tropes of sexy bad-girl rockers nor were they saccharine sweet idols. Second, the song is loud, and simply the fact that Shonen Knife was unafraid to be loud is worth noting. They are not meek performers; they insist on being heard. Finally, the topic of Barbie is significant. The lyrics outline Barbie's body parts— "blue eyes, blonde hair, tight body, long legs." Barbie's sheer foreignness alludes to an issue made apparent in the song's concluding line: "I wanna be Twist Barbie . . . *naritai na!*" (wanna become). As American culture permeated Japan throughout the twentieth century, ideal notions of beauty changed. Nowadays, many women in Japan lighten the color of their hair, use special skin-lightening make-up, and a few even undergo cosmetic surgery to make their eyes appear wider and more Caucasian. In light of both Japanese and American media's demanding physical standards, "Twist Barbie" offers a deeper investigation into the role mass culture plays in shaping notions of beauty globally, to the detriment of all women.

The song can be divided into three sections: a verse ("blue eyes, blonde hair, tight body, long legs"), a pre-chorus ("she's very smart, she's welcomed by boys, ooo, ahh"), and a chorus ("bang bang bang, Twist Barbie"). The song's harmonic palette centers on an A major scale, with the chorus utilizing the blues pentatonic scale (Biamonte 2010: 104–5). As explained by popular music theorist Nicole Biamonte, this scale is common in rock guitar and can be easily played as a box shape on the frets (Biamonte 2010: 104). This scale includes five pitches that can be designated as 1, flat 3, 4, 5, flat 7; in an A blues pentatonic scale, A is 1, C is flat 3, D is 4, E is 5, and G is flat 7, all of which can be harmonized in triads, indicated by Roman numerals. The short instrumental riff that opens "Twist Barbie" foreshadows the use of the blues pentatonic scale as the guitar alternates between A major (I) and C major (flat III) chords. The verse and pre-chorus for "Twist Barbie" follow an A major scale: the verse features the chords A major (I) and D major (IV), and the pre-chorus shifts between B minor (ii) and D major (IV). The oscillation between the B minor and D major chords, along with the ascending "ooo, ahhh" in the vocals, builds musical tension that makes the movement from the final chord of the pre-chorus, the dominant chord of E major (V), to the chorus's beginning on A (I) so satisfying. The ascending harmonies of the chorus (I-flat III-IV-V) also contribute to a sense of tension that again culminates on I. While "Twist Barbie" draws on techniques from rock-and-roll traditions, it is not as simple as it perhaps sounds. The same can be said of many other Shonen Knife tunes.

Like "Twist Barbie," "Diet Run" incorporates retro 1960s musical elements with pop punk. It too mixes English and

Japanese lyrics, indicating Shonen Knife's increasing turn outward to global fans—by 1991, they were already amassing fans outside of Japan. "Diet Run" is comprised of an ABAB-instrumental bridge-AB-tag structure. In the A sections, vocals alternate between backing voices intoning "On the diet run" and lead vocalist Naoko singing the Japanese lyrics. The bass line outlines the harmonic progression, not in the straightforward duple pattern that might be expected in a song about running, but in a dotted quarter-quarter-eighth-quarter note pattern, giving the song a sprightly, swinging feel. The tempo is not terribly fast. Together, this rhythm and speed of the song create a sense of momentum and fun. This diet run is not an all-out-until-you-drop run; it is a pleasant jog through the park while the singer envisions eating delicious foods. The singer is working to make her body healthier, but she's unlikely to give up sweets. The B section makes this clear when it begins with the line, "*dakedo tabetai*" ("but I want to eat"). While nowadays many recognize that the notion of a diet run is body-negative, here in this song the singer understands how to balance exercise and with the pleasure of eating.

"Diet Run," like "Twist Barbie," plays with harmonic ambiguity within a rock music context. The song centers on the chord C major (I), which is supported by the A sections' reiterations of G major (V) to "on the diet run" to the lyrical responses on C. The B section, though, is made of E flat and B flat major chords (flat III and flat VII) before ending up on C, indicating a C blues pentatonic scale as the guiding tonality of the song. The B section's chords serve a similar function as the G major chord in that they pull to C, but because they are flattened, they also convey a feeling of downward pressure; the lower register of the vocals in the B section adds to this feeling. The overall affect of the B section is that of heaviness that contrasts with the A section's spryness. The saxophone and guitar break down prior to the concluding verse and the chorus supports this interpretation. The instrumental interlude has an improvised feel to it; the saxophonist likely recorded an improvised solo and the guitar (played by Naoko) then doubles the line. The insertion of a sax solo into a rock song here echoes the classic Stax Records sound. The solo, in other words, marks this song as atypical of the 1990s underground rock scene just as the lyrics themselves encapsulate a particular attitude toward food, diet, and exercise.

"Heavy Song," the title track for the 2002 album *Heavy Songs*, is another rare example of a Shonen Knife food song that takes a critical approach to food consumption and body type. Its slow tempo conveys a sense of lethargy. The verses are in the key of A minor, which endows the sections with a sense of gloom. Electric organ, bass guitar, and drum set accompany the singer as she bemoans the irresistible temptation to eat cake and frets about weight gain. One line summarizes this concern as Naoko sings, "I don't want to be like the big Elvis; I must guard against being overweight." This simple couplet invokes rock history and the scrutiny public artists face regarding body image: while Shonen Knife is an indie rock band, they are not impervious to the attention they receive regarding their physical appearance. The electric organ that accompanies the verse is ominous; it aurally references a popular music history associated with the sound of radio and television villains, and the Doors, a 1960s band known for their troubled relationship with sensual temptations of a variety much harder than the heavy cream and cheesecakes beckoning Naoko. American and European listeners might hear another allusion: the organ is historically connected to Christianity. By extension the song invokes temptation and judgment of sin that pervades the religion's cultural history.

But when the bridge for "Heavy Song" kicks in with acoustic guitar, the harmony shifts to the parallel major mode of C. The singer's outlook becomes hopeful, but this optimism is fleeting. The tune ends with a clearly outlined minor chord in the organ, implying that the singer will lose her battle with temptation and give in to the siren call of the cake. The musical despondency and lyrics explicating body weight anxiety in "Heavy Song" make it a rarity in Shonen Knife's songbook. Nevertheless, it is an important piece that captures a person's fraught relationship with food that encompasses everything from clean eating to sinful bakes.[2]

Outliers

"Diet Run" and "Heavy Song" differ from the majority of Shonen Knife songs about food in that they depict body image anxiety, on one hand; "Cannibal Papaya" (Hitokui Papaya) and "Tomato Head" (*Rock Animals,* 1994), on the other hand, are unusual tunes in that are only obliquely about food. Numerous Shonen Knife songs not addressed in this book make indirect or short references to food or eating. "Banana Fish" (written by Michie and appearing on *Burning Farm* [1983]) has coloring similar to a banana and in "Elephant Pao Pao," also on *Burning Farm,* the pachyderm feels healthy (*genki*) after eating a banana. The following album, *Yama No Attchan* (1984), include the beloved "Flying Jelly Attack," an energetic track about jellybeans and cherry drops. This tune later appeared on *Let's Knife* (1992). But among these outliers, the avant-pop track "Cannibal Papaya" stands out.

The song originally appeared on Shonen Knife's first release, a homemade tape cassette album called *Everyone Have Fun* (*Minna Tanoshiku*) from 1982 and later was featured on *Yama No Attchan*.[3] "Cannibal Papaya" is comprised of a verse-chorus structure and has a scrappy, new-wave punk feel that is reminiscent of early Talking Heads. Written by Shonen Knife's original bass player Michie and in Japanese, the song's first stanza describes an idyllic life led by a group of indigenous people in South Asia. One thing troubles their peaceful existence: the fear of people-eating fruits (in addition to papayas, bananas and pineapples also pose a threat). The locals try to appease the fruit monsters but with little success. The overdriven guitar part contains a whisper of reggae that is complemented by thumping octaves in the bass during the verses. The chromatically descending choruses of "Ah ah ah ah" at the opening, along with similar vocalizations on "oh ah" after each verse-chorus structure, have a twofold function. First, the vocalizations are aesthetically in line with Shonen Knife's tendency to include moments of wordless harmony in songs, a quality clearly drawn from 1960s rock and pop style. Second, though, they also can be understood as the cries of the indigenous people Michie sings about.

What appears to be a paradise (at one point the singer wonders if the isle is heaven) is, in fact, a place of fear and mayhem. The description of a pristine South Pacific nation under a yellow sun, with blue skies, surrounded by green oceans contrasts with 1980s Japan, and especially with urban areas like Osaka. In this reference to an exotic locale, the song alludes to the growing amount of tourism in less industrialized Asian countries that were colonized and mined for resources by Japan during the Second World War. The exotification of such locations is apparent in later songs like "Banana Chips" and in Japanese popular culture more generally.[4] Given the historical context, we can understand "Cannibal Papaya" not only as a creative early Shonen Knife track but also as one that offers a subtle political commentary on consumption and in turn, being metaphorically consumed by mass culture.

"Tomato Head," another curious Shonen Knife food song, appeared on the album *Rock Animals* released in 1993 in Japan and 1994 in the United States. The inspiration for the song came while the band was touring with BMX Bandits; every night while others drank alcohol at the bar, Naoko ordered tomato juice. One BMX Bandit member teased her, warning that she would turn into a tomato from drinking so much juice (Ishihara 1993: 6). The track is one of the earliest Shonen Knife songs to receive significant airplay in the United States—a 1994 episode of MTV's *Beavis and Butt-Head* "Safe Driving" even featured the "Tomato Head" music video.[5] The infamously derisive cartoon duo did not know what to make of the video, which shows the band playing outdoors in an industrial area. Interspersed between shots of the band are people walking in suits with large tomatoes instead of human heads. Shonen Knife also performed "Tomato Head" to a bemused audience on an episode of *The Late Show with Conan O'Brien* in 1994.

By the mid-1990s, Shonen Knife was familiar with the Seattle scene, having opened for Mudhoney in Osaka and toured with Nirvana twice. In both the music video and the live performance, the band members dress in jeans and T-shirts, and Naoko wears sunglasses and a leather jacket. The style is appropriately grunge, as is the music, which brings to mind Nirvana's "Lithium." A repeated verse-verse-pre-chorus-chorus-instrumental provides the structure for the song. Backing vocals in tight harmony during the chorus appear again, solidifying the technique as quintessential to the Shonen Knife sound. The rhythmic change-ups and nuanced guitar solos also illustrate moments of musical experimentation within the standard structure and straightforward harmonies associated with grunge. What is also notable on this track is that Naoko sings in low register, the complete opposite of the stereotypical J-pop female voice. The airy backing vocals an octave above the main vocals contrast with this low range. The unison vocal line at the chorus suggests via musical metaphor that everyone has joined the singer in her obsessive desire to "be like tomato head."[6]

In the lyrics for "Tomato Head," the singer describes drinking vast quantities of tomato juice. While Naoko comments on the health aspects of tomato juice in the original 1993 Japanese version, references to its beneficial properties do not appear in the English-language release from 1994.[7] Instead the lyrics convey her insane obsessiveness with tomato juice. She admits, "Some might think I'm going mad." By the song's conclusion, the enunciating character consumes so much juice that she literally transforms into the eponymous tomato head. Taken in tandem with the music video, the lyrics paint a dark, Kafka-esque spin on the English-language adage "You are what you eat." The notion that overconsumption can physically change the body is of course nothing new, but in this song, and especially the music video, the minor-mode grunge rock and grotesque tomato head businessmen add a layer of meaning uncommon in Shonen Knife's music. There is nothing cute about the singer's tomato juice obsession; the transformation into a monstrous tomato head makes one wonder if the tomato is a metaphor for a much harder substance.

Food for Fun

While the aforementioned songs in this chapter deal with body image or indirect references to food, they are exceptions to the rule. The vast majority of Shonen Knife's food songs are upbeat, major key tracks portraying the pleasures of consumption. The sensual pleasure of eating emphasized in these songs suggests a subtle undermining of traditional gender stereotypes. Rather than being producers of food for the family, the singing female protagonists are the consumers of it. Furthermore, instead of fretting about food, the singer embraces the joy of eating. The act is a powerful one.

Among their many songs about enjoying food, one of Shonen Knife's earliest is "I Wanna Eat Choco[late] Bars" (Choko bā tabetaiyo no uta) from the 1986 album *Pretty Little Baka Guy*. It exemplifies Shonen Knife's early sound lacking overdriven guitar; the tune's texture is thinner and lighter than the band's 2010s releases. A prelude including drums, bass, guitar, and keyboard establishes the mood before Naoko's voice enters, singing "I like choco-bars" and listing ingredients in said bars. Overall, the one-minute-and-thirty-nine-second track sounds like a fusion of punk and new wave. "I Wanna Eat Chocobars," like "Diet Run," combines English and Japanese; *choko* is a common Japanese abbreviation for chocolate, and the chorus includes Japanese words expressing love and desire to eat—*daisuki* and *tabetai*. These direct statements leave little room for misinterpretation, while the song's linguistic hybridity alludes to the transnational quality of the lyrical subject, chocolate.

Originating in Mexico and making its way to Europe in the sixteenth century, chocolate had arrived in Japan by 1797 via a Dutch trading post off the coast of Nagasaki.[8] By 1868, Tokugawa Akitake, the brother of Japan's military shōgun leader, was sipping chocolate in Paris while studying abroad and taking in the world fair (Chocolate and Cocoa Association of Japan). Following the restoration of the imperial system in 1868 and push for modernization, chocolate production in Japan began in earnest, with the Morinaga company founding Japan's first chocolate factory in 1899 and selling Japan's first domestic chocolate bars in 1909 (Chocolate and Cocoa Association of Japan). Other confectionary makers like Fujiya, Akutagawa, and Tokyo Confectionary (today known as Meiji Confectionary) soon followed suit. While the importation of cocoa beans ceased during the Pacific War, chocolate production and consumption returned in full force in the postwar era. By the time of "I Wanna Eat Chocobars" in 1986, Japan had a long history of chocolate consumption and had adopted holidays centered on chocolate like Valentine's Day and White Day. Deceptively short and sweet, "I Wanna

Eat Chocobars" musically mirrors the transnational aspect of chocolate, a universal happy object, and presaged future Japanese pop songs about chocolate such as Perfume's "Chocolate Disco" *(Fan Service*, 2007) and Babymetal's "Gimme Chocolate!!" (*Babymetal*, 2015).

The 1993 track "Strawberry Cream Puff" (Ichigo shū kurīmu) continues a trend of songs about sweets. Featured on *Rock Animals* (1994), "Strawberry Cream Puff" seems a straightforward tune that harkens back to the early Beatles; it has a steady 4/4 meter and is in B major.[9] The melodic vocal line drives the tune's structure, with the verse comprised of two distinct sections that contrast with the chorus. The song is entirely in English, signaling Shonen Knife's desire to reach its new international fans and Naoko's increasing comfort with writing in English. The lyrics address the delicious pleasure of eating strawberry cream puffs, also known as "shū creams" in Japan. The singer expresses the life-changing experience of consuming her first strawberry cream puff; the memory lingers. Before encountering the delectable pastry, she was content. Now, lacking access to strawberry cream puffs, the singer relates that "every day is lonely . . . everything is boring . . . my heart is breaking . . . there is something missing in my life." Reflecting on these lyrics, they evoke the melodramatic declarations common to 1960s pop ballads such as Bobby Vinton's "I'm Mr. Lonely" from 1964. Shonen Knife avoids writing songs about love and longing for the opposite sex; instead, this musical affection is reserved for the pastry. In their music, a longing for food replaces the longing for a heteronormative romantic relationship.

But there is something even deeper happening in the song. While "Strawberry Cream Puff" remains in the carefree major mode throughout, the chorus's lyrics bittersweetly acknowledge that the object of desire (the strawberry cream puff) is unattainable. To reference the theory of French philosopher Jacques Lacan, the cream puff is the singer's *objet petit a*—part of the pleasure lies in her unrequited desire (Žižek 1991: 3–12). This longing captures another important relationship with food: that of food and memory.[10] The singer's recollection of the cream puff is idealized to the point of obsession. The dessert haunts the singer, but there is also pleasure in not fulfilling this desire. The cream puff can continue to encourage the singer to explore, imagine, and reflect on her craving. By attending to her sensual yet nonsexual urges the song's protagonist achieves a certain agency. The continual use of pronouns hints at this; while of course pronouns are commonly used in the English language, they are relatively rare in Japanese. Thus, through English, the singer can much more easily portray herself as the subject, the "I," throughout the song. The use of "my" supports this impression of an active subject. While a quirk of the English language, the effect also works with the interpretation of the song as feminist—the repeated deployment of personal pronouns here complements the subject's conscious recognition of desire and sensual fulfillment.

Pig Out!

The last two songs I examine in this chapter, "BBQ Party" (*Super Group,* 2010)" and "All You Can Eat" (*Pop Tune,* 2012), continue in this vein but feature more savory foods and even a bit of gluttony. Both songs' lyrics are entirely in English, again pointing to the band's well-established turn toward the global underground rock circuit by the early 2000s. Moreover, the songs channel specificities about food culture in Japan and the United States, respectively. "BBQ Party" features Nakanishi Etsuko on drums and Taneda Ritsuko on bass, and Naoko on guitar and vocals. The popular American song form AABA (also known as thirty-two-bar form) provides the song's foundational structure and the harmonic material is primarily limited to the three staple chords of rock and roll: A (I), D (IV), and E (V). The A sections of the song's structure feature similar musical material but different lyrical content, while the B material is both musically and lyrically differentiated. The first A section serves as an introduction; it is slower in tempo and features only unfiltered electric guitar and vocals while the following A section includes drums, bass, and overdriven guitar at a faster, hard rock pace. The A sections both begin with the same opening couplet: "Let's have a barbecue party, it's a sunny day. Let's have a barbecue party, under the cherry trees."[11]

Following this, Naoko lists different foods to grill, ranging from vegetables, marshmallows, and, to quote the song, "of course, juicy meats." The third A section is structured similarly though instead of food, the singer lists springtime creatures likes tweeting birds, buzzing bees, and butterflies. Each A section concludes on an E (V) chord that transitions back to A (I). The lack of harmonic intricacy here may compel listeners to initially assess the song as simple. Nevertheless, the transparent pull of V to I has a secondary purpose: listeners' desire for the harmonic resolution parallels the subject's desire to eat.

The lyrics for the B section clarify this. Naoko intones "pig out" nine times, urging listeners to consume with abandon. She concludes, "don't worry about your diet." Attached at the end of the thirty-two-bar structure is a repeated B section that increases in speed and volume. The frenzied coda musically paints images of feasting partygoers devouring the grilled goods.

Scrutinizing the lyrics here also reveals the tune's cross-cultural pedagogical component. Written in English, the song is presumably meant to appeal to fans across the world, including the United States. Americans accustomed to a different kind of grilling get-together might be surprised and intrigued by Naoko's description of the BBQ party. By drawing on Japanese iconography related to springtime, such as blossoming cherry trees, as well as grilled tofu and squid, Naoko imparts some cultural knowledge about Japanese barbecuing to listeners.

The final song discussed in this overview, "All You Can Eat," likewise refers to specific food culture, in this case the American buffet instead of the Japanese-style *tabehōdai*. The lyrics make this clear, with their reference to taking a plate and helping yourself to food, a characteristic specific to the American buffet. Naoko urges some temperance, reminding listeners to take some vegetables; the singer restrains herself at the buffet though her resolve seems to crumble when she encounters the tempting chocolate fountain. In other words, these lyrics combine elements from the songs about body image with songs about pleasurable consuming. The singing subject reaches a balanced, healthy relationship with food.

The musical material for "All You Can Eat" is sparse; only two main sections that I designate A and B comprise the song. The A section appears six times in conjunction with lyrics as well as in the instrumental bridge consisting of a kazoo solo. The chords A (I)–E (V)–D (IV) provide the basis for the A section's harmonies, while in the B section, the harmony slightly varies, shifting from minor vi to V/V to V (F# minor to B major to E major, then D major back to A). In this tune, too, the deceptively naive façade hints at more subtle symbolism. The consistent reiteration of the line, "all you can eat" musically harkens the numerous returns diners make to the buffet. Additionally, this song more than the others discussed in this chapter lends itself to audience participation. Clapping reminiscent of early Beatles' tunes occurs in the second A section and during live performances the bassist usually guides the audience in the snappy rhythm. The song has some other moments that lend themselves to audience participation, such as singing "all you can eat" in the song's conclusory section. At shows, Shonen Knife also sometimes sells kazoos at the merchandise table, encouraging fans to purchase one and turn the kazoo solo into a kazoo choir. Live performances of "All You Can Eat" foster a community of listener-performers.[12] This ad hoc communality in the song mirrors the communal aspect of eating whether it involves breaking bread together or sharing a pot of rice. The deft nuances of this song transform a glib pop tune into a celebration of food and community.

In sum, Shonen Knife's food-related songs generally fall into one of three categories: (1) songs about food and body image, (2) songs in which food is lyrically present, but peripheral, or (3) songs in which the singer expresses desire for food and takes pleasure in its consumption. Among these categories, the latter is by far the most common in Shonen Knife's output. Through these tunes, the band transforms the mundane action of eating into something special. The glorification of physical desire and its quenching is not a unique topic in rock and roll; what is unique is that it is food, not sexual acts, that provides sensual pleasure in the world of Shonen Knife's music. In this, the band offers a smorgasbord of songs that highlight female desire and pleasure while remaining wholesomely cute and accessible to people of all ages and backgrounds.

4 *Konnichiwa!*
An Introduction to *Happy Hour* (1998) and Its Cover Art

We made it in an unaffected way. I think it will stimulate the brain cells of the listener directly. It's the hottest album right now.

(NAOKO)

Just like the title says, it turned out to be a happy album. Have a really good time with Shonen Knife! The recording was done in Osaka and Los Angeles. It's an album that's (sic) everyone would love and really cool.

(MICHIE)

It's a reckless explosion of power that will make you think of early Shonen Knife. You'll miss out on something if you don't give it a listen!

(ATSUKO)

These quotes from the original members of Shonen Knife appear in the book *Shonen Knife Land* that was published concomitant with the release of *Happy Hour* (1998: 72). The release of the book and album represents the culmination of an era in Shonen Knife's career. Shonen Knife recorded the fourteen-song album on the heels of their hugely successful

"Blast Off Tour" in the United States in 1997.[1] While the band had steadily received positive press, they were still having to budget studio time; each song on *Happy Hour* was fully formed by the time they began recording at a studio in Osaka, with some of the drum tracks recorded in Hollywood (Yamano Naoko, interview with the author, July 16, 2018, Osaka). The original Japanese release featured both the English tracks and Japanese-language versions of the songs "Cookie Day," "Sushi Bar Song," "Banana Chips," "Dolly," and "People Traps" (Otoshi Ana). By this time, they were being distributed by Universal Victor, which allowed them to reach a wider audience. In addition to the Japanese release, the album was also distributed in Europe and Australia on compact disc and on tape cassette in the Philippines (the Australia and Philippines releases included the Japanese version of "Banana Chips" as a bonus track). Big Deal Records distributed *Happy Hour* in the United States and its promo disc included one track that did not make it onto the final album, "Huge Snail," a song penned by Michie (George Handlon, email communication, August 6, 2019). A cover of the Monkees' tune "Daydream Believer" caps off the American release of the album. The band used technology to reach its global fan community early on; as part of the promotion for *Happy Hour*, Shonen Knife performed a live-streamed show from Microsoft Studios in Seattle, Washington.[2] Following the album's release, the group embarked on Wonder Tour '98, playing in cities around Japan and concluding with a performance at the famous Fuji Rock Festival on August 1 (Handlon 1998: 8). After the festival, Shonen Knife toured the United States and Canada. Shortly thereafter, original bassist Michie resigned to have time to herself. The first era of Shonen Knife came to an end, and the band was at a crossroads: to continue or quit. *Happy Hour* thus marks an important midpoint in Shonen Knife's career in terms of its lineup, image, and music.

The late 1990s were also an important turning point for the album artist Nara Yoshitomo, whose breakthrough came around the release of the *Happy Hour*. In addition to designing the cover art for Shonen Knife album, he also provided the cover art for Yoshimoto Banana's *Argentine Hag* (2002). Like Nara, whose art is in some ways connected to manga and comic book imagery, Yoshimoto's writing style is frequently associated with the stories of girls' manga, known as *shōjo* manga. The aesthetic connection between Yoshimoto and Nara runs deeper though; both have an affinity for punk music, both artists feature female characters that seem initially shallow but contain great depth, and simplicity imbues a deep interiority in its subjects. This is as true of Nara's artwork as it is of Yoshimoto's *Kitchen* (a 1988 novella centered on food and relationships), and Shonen Knife's music. There are a few other shared qualities among these three types of artists (literary, visual, musical): they are of the same generation, and they are incredibly prolific. These artists operated in a shared *Zeitgeist* and a common thread connects the works of Yoshimoto, Nara, and Shonen Knife. That common thread is punk and a combination of the cute with the cool.

Nara Yoshitomo: Artist as Punk

Nara, like his fellow visual artist and friend Murakami Takashi, is a leading Japanese neo-pop artist who is internationally known.

However, Nara is considerably more introspective; his work, often depicting small children and animals (mostly dogs) in solitary settings, evokes a melancholy aura (Trescher 2001: 9–10). Some of this aura might have a connection to Nara's background. He was born in 1959 in Hirosaki, a city in rural Aomori Prefecture in northern Japan. Nara's birthplace is significant; he is not from a cosmopolitan center such as Tokyo or Osaka. In an interview with Stephan Trescher, Nara related that "In the area I'm from[,] there was no museum—and there still isn't. I received my visual stimuli more from television, from Japanese and American comic books, and from European children's books. That's why comic books have a greater reality for me than the European painting that I later came to know and study intensively" (Nara and Trescher 2001: 104). While in some ways isolating, the other result of a rural upbringing was that there were fewer influences judging and guiding a child's imagination. This free creativity helped him to deal with some of the loneliness that came from both of Nara's parents working. A rich imagination staved off solitude and also cultivated a self-reliance that would extend into a sense of punk-inflected DIY creativity that remains apparent in his work today.

Nara's style is at once utterly simple and brimming with depth, making it visually analogous to Shonen Knife's music. Many of his images feature simple designs of solitary subjects with round features; most appear to be dolls. Marilyn Ivy describes these subjects: Nara's "signature characters, the ones that seem to exemplify this aesthetic more than others, are the glaring, large-eyed girl children of his iconic portraits, strange permutations of the round-eyed, *über*-cute girls of manga and anime renown" (Ivy 2010: 7). However, Nara's children are not afraid or demure; frequently they are tough and rebellious, sometimes smoking (*Smoking Girl*), wielding a knife (*Slash with a Knife*), or telling the viewer "fuck you" (*Dead Flower*). The girls of Nara's world rarely smile, unless it is in violent joy or in peaceful repose. In this way, elements of rebellion not only are apparent in Nara's rejection of both traditional art school techniques; they are also apparent in his continued portrayal of the girl child, a figure that suggests a lack of power or agency, and thus someone with the most to gain from rebellion and the undermining of existing power structures. Nara's juxtaposition of the *kawaii* with toughness and even violence (what Ivy calls *bukimi*, or uncanny) within the subject of a female child resonates with Shonen Knife's own image as both cute and tough (Ivy 2010: 15–16). Although they are not what Ivy considers *bukimi*, a similar irony enriches their music.

Music and Image

Nara's DIY attitude, his studiously unpolished drawing style, and his consistent championing of underdogs in his visual works all clarify how the aesthetic of punk emerges in his art. Beyond this, music, and particularly punk, directly influences Nara. Nara is an avid music listener, having sought out recordings of classical music, soul, roots and blues, folk music, and of course rock during his teenage years in the mid-1970s (Nara 2017: 234). By his second year of high school, he was helping to build and decorate a rock café and visiting the local live house every weekend, sometimes acting as a DJ (Nara 2017: 235). Nara was steeped in local music and arts culture, chatted with college students older than him, and developed the scrappy attitude required for artistic misfits living in relatively rural areas. When he went on to study at art school, Nara maintained deep ties to music and arts subcultures (Nara 2017: 240).

Like Shonen Knife, Nara has an affinity for the Ramones and the band's heartfelt unvirtuosic music, something he referred to as "the beginner's spirit" in the 2010–11 New York Asia Society exhibit *Yoshitomo Nara Nobody's Fool*.[3] This beginner's spirit is at the core of Nara's work, Shonen Knife's music, and punk's DIY values in general. In an interview with Trescher, Nara related, "I came into contact with punk—this music struck a nerve and penetrated me deeply. It matched the way I was feeling at the time and I have remained true to punk" (Nara and Trescher 2001: 105). As a result, punk culture affected Nara, and its sway is evident in his works, which sometimes include references to musicians (Guitar Wolf) or song lyrics (such as David Bowie's "Rock and Roll Suicide"). Beyond that, Nara frequently collaborates with bands like Star Club, Bloodthirsty Butchers, and Noodles on album covers. His affinity for music makes Nara especially attuned to the relationship between music and image. The interaction between sound and image in the cover of Shonen Knife's *Happy Hour* exemplifies how the visual artist and band amplify each other's aesthetic.

Interestingly, *Happy Hour* was not the first album depicting the female band members of dolls; 1996's *Brand New Knife* depicts the musicians as cute, brightly hued stuffed bunny rabbits playing their respective rock-and-roll instruments. In that cover art, the band capitalizes on the iconographic juxtaposition between the hyper-cute and cool, and by extension, comments on gender and stereotypes related to the rock world more broadly. They are women musicians transformed into cute stuffed animals. The same holds true in Nara's artwork for Shonen Knife, which varies slightly between the American release and the Japanese one. *Happy Hour* features several songs about food, so it seems natural that in the American release, Nara's drawing of the doll-like girl, presumably Naoko, is clutching lollipops as if waving two flags. In the American version, the album title appears in rainbow lettering around the lollipops. The words seem to form a halo around the candy, linking the words "happy hour" to the sticky sweet treat favored by children. One can extrapolate that the music will be equally sweet. The artwork for the back of the album features Atsuko and Michie proxies holding drumsticks and a bass guitar respectively. The Michie figure is even smiling. In the album art for the Japanese release, the young subject holds a guitar in one hand and a lollipop proudly in the other, again as if implying that the music and candy are one. The girl does not smile and her sideways glance is more defiant than those that appear on the American cover. It is easy to imagine the subject as a relative to the Powerpuff Girls both in terms of design and spirit.

These images reference a sketch Nara did for the album artwork, now held by the Museum of Modern Art in New York City. This sketch provides greater insight into the doll image and its connection to the band; in this image, Nara depicts the girl actually playing guitar, her mouth opened in a singing "oh," eyes closed as if she is lost in the musical moment. The seeming simplicity of the drawing, with its rough pencil sketching and crayon strokes, indicates something deeper about not only Nara's relationship to art but also Shonen Knife's relationship to music. The sketch establishes the cute doll with the cool red

Image 4.1 *Nara Yoshitomo's sketch for the cover of* Happy Hour. *Nara, Yoshitomo (b. 1959) Copyright. Happy Hour/Shonen Knife 1992–2000. Crayon and pencil on paper, 4 ¾ x 4 ¾" (12.1x12.1 cm). Gift of David Teiger in honor of Agnes Gund. Digital Image Copyright The Museum of Modern Art/Licensed by SCALA/Art Resource, NY].*

electric guitar as an iconographic incarnation of Shonen Knife's music while also capturing the band's unstudied sincerity. But most importantly, the girl is at peace while singing and playing. In this, the sketch captures what many *josei* rockers around the world have likely felt at one point or another: playing music, whether alone, in a small club, or rock arena, is a vehicle for transcendence. We can close our eyes, escape the outside world, and let ourselves be comfortable abandoning the gendered dichotomy of cute and cool (see Image 4.1).

5 *Happy Hour*
Food, Music, and Transnational Flow

Food, like Shonen Knife's music, exemplifies a transnational flow. By this term, I mean the exchange of cultural commodities, ideas, and values between countries in a feedback loop. This kind of flow is especially apparent in exchanges between Japan and the United States. Sushi provides an excellent example. Traditional Japanese sushi usually features raw fish, which can be wrapped in rice and seaweed (*maki-zushi*), scattered over rice (*chirashi-zushi*), or simply placed on a bite-size oblong lump of rice (*nigiri-zushi*). As Japan played a greater role in the global economy, its cuisine made its way to mainland United States (Hawaii has a long and distinct relationship with Japanese cuisine).[1] As sushi circulated from coastal cities like Los Angeles and New York City inland to more suburban and rural locations, ingredients and combinations evolved; for example, the famous "Philly roll," a smoked salmon and cream cheese *maki-zushi*, is popular in the United States but unheard of in Japan.

But the circulation and transformation of sushi goes both ways. In the years following the Second World War, Spam was a popular meat source in both the United States and

Japan, as it was cheap and had a long shelf life. As a result of a long presence of Japanese culture as well as U.S. military in Hawaii, local nutritionist Barbara Funamura developed a tasty *o-nigiri* (rice ball) that incorporated Spam (Fujimoto 2016). The concoction known as Spam *musubi* is now popular not only in Hawaii (it is said to be the favorite snack of the state's famous son Barack Obama) but also in Japan, especially Okinawa (Jones 2014; Koikari 2018). Other examples of this kind of transnational flow include anime; Disney films influenced Japanese artists like Miyazaki Hayao, whose works in turn influenced Pixar movies. Music functions similarly. While it can be said that rock and roll originated in the United States, it is by no means restricted geographically as a cultural art form. As popular music circulates, it informs other artists around the world, who, in turn, influence others. So how does this concept of transnational flow relate to Shonen Knife's *Happy Hour*? "Sushi Bar Song," "Gyoza," "Hot Chocolate," and "Cookie Day" present different means of understanding this phenomenon.

Singing the Nation: "Sushi Bar Song" and "Gyoza"

"Sushi Bar Song" and "Gyoza" demonstrate transnational flow: both songs reference the foods' origins (Japan and China respectively), and both were recorded in English. Even the Japanese version of "Sushi Bar Song" contains several English loanwords. While the two songs lyrically and sometimes musically reference the national, the use of the English language and rock instrumentation adds a patina of the globalism to the tracks. English's materialization in Japanese popular music more broadly has to do simply with the sounds of words and a desire for a cosmopolitan veneer. In a 1997 interview with *Big O* magazine, Naoko related that she generally writes songs in English first and then translates them into Japanese (Lim, Horn, and Harrison 1997: 21–2). "I think English is not only a language for American people or British people. It's the language of rock'n' roll," she said (Lim, Horn, and Harrison 1997: 22). While many of Shonen Knife's albums in the 1980s and 1990s featured a combination of Japanese and English tracks, the group has written almost exclusively in English since 2008, though they perform in Japanese at live shows in Japan. The band's sustained popularity and desire to be accessible to fans outside of Japan explains this linguistic decision in part. The increase in English-language tunes also hints at the members', and especially Naoko's, comfort in navigating a musical path between the Japanese indie rock scene and the global one. The *Happy Hour* tracks recorded in both English and Japanese demonstrates Naoko's keen awareness of the relationship between music and text.

"Sushi Bar Song" offers an interesting glimpse into this relationship. Unlike "Cookie Day," discussed later, few differences exist between the English and Japanese versions of the tune. Part of this has to do with the fact that names of sushi fish comprise the majority of the verses' lyrics, and the chorus of both the versions is in English: "Sushi, sushi, sushi bar, going to a sushi bar." Also notable is that "Sushi Bar Song" is about a nutritious food instead of a tempting dessert. If, as suggested in Chapter 3, Shonen Knife's numerous songs about sweets are a means of rebelling against the etiquette of healthy eating and dieting, then what might a song about something nutritious like sushi signify?

In the song, the line "healthy menu" appears in both versions, as does the line "beautiful Japanese meal" (in the Japanese, the English word "food" appears instead of "meal"). The adjectives "healthy" and "Japanese" are repeated in the second verse as well. The linking of healthy and Japanese has many implications that conjure nationalist discourse. For example, Japan's government promotes a food education campaign aimed at building and maintaining a healthy citizenry, first while they are students, and later as adults. Indeed, the 2005 *shokuiku* (nutritional education) law emphasized the preparation of healthy Japanese cuisine and its connection to an imagined, idealized rural lifestyle, declaring: "Awareness and appreciation of traditional Japanese food culture as well as food supply/demand situations should be promoted, and opportunities of interaction between food producers and consumers should be created, in order to revitalize rural farming and fishing regions, and to boost food self-sufficiency in Japan" (Ministry of Agriculture, Forestry, and Fisheries 2005: 3). While the informational packet promoting *shokuiku* does not explicitly blame foreign fast food for Japanese diet woes, the images feature traditional staples like rice, miso soup, and fish, front and center.[2] "Snacks, confections, and beverages" should be enjoyed moderately according to guidelines; such items have no place in the *shokuiku* dietary "spinning top," akin to the United States' food pyramid (Ministry of Agriculture, Forestry, and Fisheries 2005: 7).

Additionally, it is especially up to parents, educators, and daycare providers to promote *shokuiku* to children. Again, the implication is obvious though not stated outright—it is primarily up to women in their roles as mothers, elementary school teachers, and caregivers to nourish Japan's children properly.[3] The explanatory pamphlet hammers this point home by concluding with an image of a group of smiling schoolgirls showing off healthy *o-bento* they made (Ministry of Agriculture, Forestry, and Fisheries 2005: 10). In this, the current food preparation education echoes imperial-era (1868–1945) ideas of "good wives and wise mothers" cooking healthy, Japanese-style meals for their families (Cwiertka 2006: 87–98, 114).[4] The soft power of food and food education can communicate very serious concepts about nationalism (Horiguchi 2018: 242).

Of course, Shonen Knife does not promote nationalist ideology in "Sushi Bar Song," but it is interesting to consider the deeper implications of what on the surface seems to be a simple song about raw fish. For example, from a cultural perspective it is worth noting that in Japan, sushi chefs are almost exclusively male.[5] In "Sushi Bar Song," a singing female subject, "I," consumes food ostensibly prepared by male chefs; even though sushi is considered a national cuisine, the centering of a woman in the public sphere eating food prepared by men represents a kind of reversal of domestic gender roles. The song's enunciator acquires a certain agency by getting to pick from all the menu options prepared by the male sushi chefs.

The frequent embedding of English loanwords in the Japanese version of the song is a lyrical metaphor for the transnationality of the "world famous Japanese food." The chorus, which is sung in harmony by Shonen Knife and the

1990s alternative rock band the Presidents of the United States of America suggests an exchange that is musical as well as linguistic. Finally, the use of English is an inconspicuous hint at the inspiration for "Sushi Bar Song," a little sushi restaurant in Dallas, Texas. In our chat, Naoko related that the band went there during a tour, and they found it surprisingly decent. The only issue was that instead of serving miso soup with the meal, as is common in Japan, the soup was served before the main course. She also noted that green tea was served with the sushi course at the Dallas restaurant as it is in Japan (Yamano N., interview).[6] Green tea's anti-bacterial powers also make it an important post-sushi beverage (Yamano N., email communication, August 14, 2020). Throughout, "Sushi Bar Song" subtly addresses transnational gastro-diplomacy, gender roles, cultural education, and musical exchange.

These issues emerge in the music itself. The opening chorus along with the driving drum set beating on one-two-and-three-four together evokes California beaches and the music of the Beach Boys, or more closely the Go-Go's. After the opening chorus, electric guitar and lead vocals by Naoko enter the mix. She sings directly to the listener in both versions, inviting them to eat sushi together. The harmony, though, is less direct. In the first half of the stanza, the standard pop harmonic progression of I (A), IV (D), and V (E) is followed by a minor vi chord (F-sharp minor) rather than the expected return to I, creating what is called a deceptive cadence. It makes our ears hungry for the expected harmonic resolution of V to I. In the verse's conclusion, Naoko provides us listeners not only with the craved "aural meal" of the authentic cadence of V to I, she also wets our appetite for sushi by mentioning delectable ingredients like octopus (*tako*), shrimp (*ebi*), fatty tuna (*toro*), and fermented soy beans (*nattō*). Musical and gastronomic desires deliciously merge.

The verse's litany of sushi types also has an illustrative function. The names of the fish seem to parade across our mind's eye. It is as if the sushi dishes are slowly proceeding down a conveyor belt at a *kaiten-zushi* restaurant, a gimmick that first appeared in Shonen Knife's hometown, Osaka, in 1958 (Cwiertka 2006: 191). The cyclic structure of the song (a chorus, verse, and bridge that repeats) formally reflects the round path of the sushi conveyor belt while the steady drum beat musically renders the sound of the belt's rotation. While *kaiten-zushi* bars are not considered high-class, since the 1990s these kinds of restaurants have become places where families, students, women, and couples on a budget can go to enjoy the traditional food (Cwiertka 2006: 193–4). Shonen Knife's songs provide a similar space, making elements of Japanese culture, both culinary and musical, accessible to all types of people.

Like "Sushi Bar Song," "Gyoza" also addresses the connections between nation, music, and food. Commonly known as pot stickers in the United States, Chinese *jiaozi* are small dumplings usually filled with a combination of minced meat and vegetables. They can be fried, boiled, or steamed and are an especially popular dish at Chinese New Year. Japanese soldiers returning from China following the Second World War introduced *gyōza* to their home country. Thus, *gyōza*, like many other popular dishes in Japan, including ramen noodles and *man* (steamed buns filled with either sweet bean paste or savory meats), serve as a contemporary reminder of Japan's long and complicated history with mainland China. *Gyōza* thus make for a thorny lyrical topic.

Shonen Knife's "Gyoza" aurally portrays the dumplings' Chinese origins. The song features some musical markers that Western composers have historically employed to emphasize the exotic. Musicians ranging from Mozart to Carl Douglas (of "Kung Fu Fighting" fame) deployed these markers as a way of depicting an imagined version of a foreign land. Edward Said theorized this phenomenon and its proliferation throughout Western culture, postulating that Western artists have historically treated the East as a fantasy object (Said 1979: 67–8). Said calls this process of presenting an imagined, inaccurate version of a foreign culture "Orientalism." The problem with Orientalism lies in its simultaneous mystification and objectification of non-Western cultures, even when these non-Western cultures are presented in a positive light.

"Gyoza" borrows some of Western music's Orientalist codes.[7] It opens with a pentatonic (five-tone) melody in parallel fourths, played by a guitar. These parallel fourths are a stereotypical shorthand for "Asia," apparent in songs like David Bowie's "China Girl" and the Vapors' "Turning Japanese." A gong reverberates as the plucked melody resolves to its tonic, E. From the outset, this prelude musically indicates "East Asia." What might be confusing for Western listeners accustomed to musical Orientalism is that from their perspective, this melody could just as easily signify Japan as it could China. However, from a Japanese perspective, it seems representative of China. But this pentatonic prelude also functions as an Orientalist gesture, marking China as "the East" and Japan in the position of "the West." As such, embedded in "Gyoza" is an intra-Asia Orientalism.[8] Yet the opening passage and the song itself are more complex than this simple binarism. By adopting Western classical and popular music's exoticist techniques and incorporating them into a song about *gyōza*, Shonen Knife invites a critical and even ironic interpretation of Orientalist stereotypes. This act is augmented by the fact that the band recorded "Gyoza" only in English, suggesting that the target of this song is English-speaking listeners. In appropriating foreign musical stereotypes, Shonen Knife leans into Orientalism. In "Gyoza," the band reclaims agency over the musical portrayal of East Asia and Japan's place within it via a combination of these generic tropes with pop punk.[9]

The structure of "Gyoza" is straightforward. A binary AB song structure follows the opening material; the music then repeats. The A and B sections feature the typical overdriven guitar, bass, and drums in addition to the vocals. In the A portion, a second guitar part emphasizes the offbeats, endowing the song with a ska edge. The blue-note-inflected melody adorns lyrics that describe the delicious *gyōza* fillings. This all changes during the B section, as does the song's texture. As Naoko sings of the *gyōza* and China's history, the drum set switches to a tom-heavy beat; the harmony and melody enter a stable major mode with a final cadence. At the end of the song, Naoko shouts "it's tasty history" as overdriven guitar and a gong reverberate. The lingering sounds hint that while the process of importing *gyōza* to Japan took place long ago, the past continues to be part of the present in the form of food.

Singing and Sweets: "Hot Chocolate" and "Cookie Day"

"Hot Chocolate" and "Cookie Day" also exhibit qualities indicative of transnational flow: both hot chocolate and cookies are associated with Western sweets, and both tunes feature a large number of English loanwords, with "Hot Chocolate" recorded exclusively in English and "Cookie Day" in both English and Japanese.[10] "Hot Chocolate" illustrates musico-lyrical fusion by painting a musical impression of the beverage. The song can be parsed into three sections: A, B, and a chorus on the word "melting," with a guitar solo and instrumental breakdown punctuating these sections. The A section begins with an overdriven guitar bounced between the left and right channels; the effect adds a spatialization to the tune, making it sound as if there are two guitars in a call-and-response pattern. In the first stanza, the singer opens with the word "hot chocolate," followed by a description of the drink.

A shift to IV (F), along with the drums moving to the ride cymbal and a flange effect on the guitar, demarcates the B section. The swimming reverb of the guitar reinforces the lyrics, which compare the melting chocolate to a tidal wave, and invites listeners to "jump in, take a swim!" After the B section, the chorus enters. It initiates with the first syllable of "melting" repeated eight times in a descending melodic pattern before the word is uttered in its entirety. By breaking down the word "melting," the first syllable becomes more musical; its textual cohesiveness dissolves just like the chocolate itself. A guitar solo follows, its climax defined by an extended repetition of a three-note ascending half-step pattern (Bb-B-C). This three-note pattern is juxtaposed against the duple-meter drumbeat, as if the rhythmic flow was a swirling mug of hot chocolate. An instrumental breakdown occurs after a reiteration of the B section's vocal line. The electric guitar and drums drop out completely, leaving the bass guitar to play the harmonic root notes C–E–A–G. It is the musical portrayal of reaching the bottom of one's mug of hot chocolate with only the dredges remaining. The rhythm guitar enters and four bars later the lead vocals come in, singing, "hot chocolate." Layers of vocal harmonies enter on the following repetitions, as if a mug is being refilled with the ingredients of hot chocolate. This additive musical process evokes standard rock practices of a breakdown and buildup; for example, the Who's "Baba O'Riley" (*Who's Next*, 1971) employs this technique. Here in "Hot Chocolate," the process gestures to rock history while also enabling the band to imbue it with their own meaning and aesthetic; instead of bemoaning lost youth like the Who, Shonen Knife's song relishes the present and the simple pleasure of sipping hot cocoa.

Conversely, "Cookie Day" does not paint a musical picture of the treat or its consumption. Instead, the bumptious ska-inflected song bespeaks a deft linguistic navigation. "Cookie Day" was recorded in both English and Japanese. A comparison of the two iterations of "Cookie Day" illuminates this process of translation and adaptation by Naoko from a song for Japanese audiences to a song for English-speaking ones. When I spoke with Naoko about this issue, she made clear that she is well-versed in the various issues of music and translation. She even cited familiarity with the early twentieth-century composer

Yamada Kōsaku, who expounded on setting the Japanese language to Western-style music. Her deep knowledge of all kinds of music helps her cultivate a sensitive approach to text translation. Naoko related that years ago, she would translate the lyrics herself and then have an English-speaking friend look them over, though nowadays she is confident about writing in English on her own (Yamano N., interview). *Happy Hour*, with several of its tracks recorded in both languages, displays Naoko's unique linguistic intuition. "Cookie Day" confirms this assessment.

Both the Japanese and English versions of "Cookie Day" trace the evolution of a mundane afternoon into an energetic musical adventure. The Japanese version of the song features some English lines, as apparent in the opening "sugar, sugar candy" and the eponymous "cookie day." The singer describes a lazy hot afternoon; she is bored and decides to make cookies. In the second verse, the singer imagines herself on vacation at the beach with a friend, bringing the homemade cookies with her. The imagery here of a beach and sun in conjunction with cookies is an unexpected one. It is as if the cookie might work as an edible talisman, transporting the singer and her friend from the quotidian to the elysian where one never worries (*nayandeitemo hajimaranai*).

The English version conveys this same light-hearted everydayness slightly differently. The first verse's lyrics are a series of thoughts that cross the singer's mind while she's bored at home watching television, which includes eating cookies and dipping them in milk, an activity common in the United States but rare in Japan. In the second verse, the singer relates that she bought a postcard while on tour in North

Dakota and it features buffalo. The references specifically to the United States here suggest that some of the ideas for the lyrics originated from the band's experiences in America the previous year. The following lines express a general optimism about life; the singer tells her listener, "There are many pretty things in life. Take it easy. Let it be." The exhortation references the attitude Paul McCartney expressed in the song "Let It Be" (*Let It Be,* 1970) as well as the Eagles' "Take It Easy" (*Eagles*, 1972). The line echoes a sentiment found in a later track on *Happy Hour*, "Catch Your Bus." In that tune as well, the singer tells the listener not to worry about missing the bus; there will, she points out, be another and everything will be fine.

The result of recording "Cookie Day" in two languages is that the music varies slightly between versions. Overall, the English version's vocal part contains more rhythmic activity than the Japanese version; Naoko employs a pattern of a sixteenth note followed by a dotted eighth note on many of the English lines. But the English version's setting of "North Dakota" stands out as a significant departure from the Japanese vocal part; the "Dakota" is set to what feels like a single set of quarter-note triplets. These discrepancies are all the more interesting because rhythmically, the English version is more difficult to sing. In recording "Cookie Day" in both English and Japanese, Naoko displays an understated virtuosity that has as much to do with her ability to sense the poetry's musicality as the music's poetic attributes.

Such talents helped Shonen Knife translate their aesthetic into international success in indie rock. Their music, like many of the foods they sing about, exemplifies the transnational flow of culture. Shonen Knife takes the ingredients of rock, a musical genre historically associated with masculinity, and cooks up something specific to their experiences as female Japanese musicians. Their association with Nirvana in the early 1990s allowed them to build an international fan base, to the degree that 1998's *Happy Hour* was marketed globally, with songs recorded in both English and Japanese and an online performance sponsored by Microsoft in the early days of the internet (Tanaka 1998: 19). With so many of *Happy Hour*'s songs featuring food, the lyrics were able to appeal across cultures while subtly commenting from a feminist point of view. In both "Sushi Bar Song" and "Gyoza," the band navigates ideas of national identity and positioning relevant to 1998, an era on the cusp of a global economic shift. "Hot Chocolate" and "Cookie Day" highlight sweets as happy objects with universal charm. This accessible allure is true of many Shonen Knife numbers recorded in both English and Japanese, including the *Happy Hour* single "Banana Chips," discussed in the following chapter.

6 The Delicious Banality of "Banana Chips"

Banana Chips, banana chips, banana chips, banana chips, banana chips, banana chips, banana chips... oh yeah!
(CHORUS TO "BANANA CHIPS")

"Banana Chips," the single from *Happy Hour*, remains standard repertoire at Shonen Knife's live shows. The song pays homage to the bands most influential to Shonen Knife—the Ramones and the Beatles—without mimicking either. With regards to the former, repetition and end phrases with "oh yeah" allude to the Ramones songs like "Beat on the Brat." The hand clapping, in tandem with the recurring guitar riff and sophisticated harmonies, evokes the Beatles. While the chorus's repetitive lyrics make the song seem simple like "Beat on the Brat," "Banana Chips" represents a complex nexus of values and ideas expressed through music, lyrics, and cultural references. Shonen Knife takes elements of rock and roll's past and tailors them to express an aesthetic specific to them, one that is simultaneously cute and cool. The band walks a fine line between earnest seriousness and tongue-in-cheek play; the members are certainly aware of the stereotypes they face, both at home as women who play rock instruments and abroad as Asian female rockers. In "Banana Chips," they embrace these stereotypes and by leaning into cuteness, Shonen Knife elevates the everyday.

If the song's cuteness derives from the superficially vapid lyrics about eating banana chips and the repetitive harmony and melody, then the cool aspect comes from the absurdity of the repetitions and the music's timbral and harmonic components. Historically, cultural theorists like Theodor Adorno have critiqued popular music for its use of repetition in large-scale form and smaller musical units (though classical music likewise uses standardized formal structures and musical units; Adorno 1941/2002: 437–69). Yet for Adorno, popular music's greatest sin is that it encourages passive listening. To him, this mindless musical consumption mirrors the passivity of citizens blindly consuming products under a capitalist regime. Several music scholars have challenged Adorno's reading of popular music. Richard Middleton, for example, points out that the repetition of short bits of musical material alludes to pop music's origins in jazz and rhythm-and-blues, genres rooted in Black music traditions (Middleton 1983: 252–61). Middleton describes how repetition (what he calls "musematic techniques"), particularly riffs, can actually provide a framework for creative development (Middleton 1983: 252–3). Moreover, repetition in popular music can be a source of individual listening pleasure that becomes a vehicle for agency rather than a sign of mass-market manipulation (Middleton 1983: 261–4). I suggest that both Adorno's and Middleton's understanding of musical repetition are relevant to Shonen Knife's "Banana Chips." The song's repetitive chorus can be understood as a representation of cultural practices of consumerism at the heart of Japan's economy. But these repetitions might also represent a self-conscious commentary on consumerism, located within a certain pleasure in the banal. In repetition, there is also the pleasure of familiar recognition of musical and lyrical patterns. The idea, to quote the "Banana Chips" lyrics, is "just a little bit sweet."

Music and Lyrics: More than Just a Banana (Chip)

"Banana Chips" imparts this aesthetic of repetition via its music, translation, and video. "Banana Chips" is not as structurally straightforward as one might think. It begins with a V chord (E major) rather than the tonic chord (A major), the V chord accompanying "Banana chips for you" as if it were a musical question waiting to be answered. The answer, "Banana chips for me," is accompanied by a I chord. This relationship between the question and answer, or antecedent and consequent phrases, drives the song's melodic and harmonic momentum. By beginning the verse on V, listeners immediately desire the resolution to I. This musical desire in turn parallels the singer's desire for banana chips (and possibly the growing cravings of the listener as well). The repetitive aspect of the musical structure and the chorus lyrics borders first into the frivolous and then into the absurd. The cyclic nature of the I–IV–V harmonic progression in the chorus reflects a never-ending cycle of musical desire and resolution. The music works as a metaphor for the simple craving of banana chips and the fulfillment of that desire, only to find yourself opening a second bag of the delectable snack a moment later.

Like many other songs appearing on *Happy Hour*, Shonen Knife recorded "Banana Chips" in both English and Japanese. Both incarnations' lyrics express a sincere joy in consuming banana chips, though similar to the translation of "Cookie Day," some lyrical meanings diverge in significant ways. For example, in the Japanese version of "Banana Chips," the treat originates in a far-off southern country. In this version, the singer also explains that banana chips are typically tucked away in a corner near the chocolate at grocery stores. However, the English version does convey the singer's insatiable desire for the snack. Instead of the dangerous obsessiveness of "Tomato Head," the desire for banana chips is celebrated in major-mode lightheartedness akin to "I Wanna Eat Chocobars" discussed in Chapter 3. "Banana Chips" luxuriates in a bodily but cute desire that is *not* sexual, as is clear by the words and the band's performance style.[1] Shonen Knife couches female longing in the "safe" vessel of the banana chip and wraps it in a blanket of repetitive rock-and-roll musical tropes. It is its own form of genius—cute, cool, and fun.

Blending Bananas: Recording and Remixes

"Banana Chips" also appears on Shonen Knife's live albums *Live in Osaka* (2006) and *ALIVE! In Osaka* (2018) and was the band's entry on the compilation album for Fuji Rock 1998, which also included Nick Cave and the Bad Seeds, Iggy Pop, and other artists. The appearance of Shonen Knife on this album marked their admittance into a wider rock world, not only in Japan but also globally and historically. And in true J-pop fashion, "Banana Chips" accompanied the end credits to the anime *Mii Fa Pū*.[2] Among the various incarnations of "Banana Chips," the three remixes of the single are relevant to this chapter's investigation into repetition and its meaning.

Universal Victor released the "Banana Chips" single in Japan in 1998. It consists of the Japanese-language recording of the track and three remixes of the song—the EY3 Mix by Yamatsuka Ai of the Boredoms; "Bomb Dub Mix" by DJ Oasis and rapper K Dub Shine (both members of the Japanese hip-hop trio King Giddra); and "Kenji Sato Mix" by Satō Kenji and Shimada Masanori.[3] Before digging into the specifics of these remixes, I want to consider the album art. As discussed in Chapter 4, the cover art for *Happy Hour* complements the album's musical qualities; this is equally true of the single's artwork. The image, drawn by Naoko, seems to be done in oil pastels, which creates a similar texture as crayons but allows for better layering and blending. Roughly drawn brown and green strokes give curvature to an image of the oblong fruit. The banana floats on a pink background with blue, yellow, and white highlights. The fruit almost seems to glow. "BANANA CHIPS" hovers in bright red English capital letters. "Shonen Knife" appears along the bottom in green. The second "N" in "Banana" is reversed, as if written by a young child still mastering her letters. The combination of the rough marks and misaligned letter endows the picture with a youthful naivety. In a conversation with Naoko, she confirmed that this was a conscious decision; she pointed out that the style of this cover art references the crayon drawings that appear as album art for Shonen Knife's *Burning Farm* (1983) and *Yama No Attchan* (1984) (Yamano N., interview). In this way, the "Banana Chips" single iconographically alludes to Shonen Knife's past. It also references rock and punk history more generally. Naoko's drawing brings to mind Andy Warhol's banana print for the Velvet Underground's debut album, *The Velvet Underground and Nico* (1967). While the single's title and artwork reflect on the past, the remixes gesture toward potential futures that play with the genres of techno as well as sound art.

EY3 Mix

The EY3 Mix deconstructs the single's musical components and incorporates samples of select tracks into a new sound collage The remix opens with samples of the hand claps and drums from the original recording and combines these samples with new material, most distinctly a jaw harp solo that soon becomes a jaw harp duet. The melodica, an instrument associated with elementary school music class in Japan, intones airy dissonant notes. Harp, sleigh bells, and the wobbly sound of shaking sheets of plastic float in and out of the mix. A wordless voice hums a melody vaguely reminiscent of the vocal line for Nirvana's "In Bloom." A small excerpt of the original track's bass line cuts in before a return to the remix's opening combination. The guitar riff from "Banana Chips" briefly appears around forty-five seconds into the track, fades away, and returns at 3:30 on loop. The second time the guitar emerges, it is as if the riff is on a skipping record. The original song haunts the EY3 Mix but never manifests. The combination of different musical textures and styles transforms "Banana Chips" into sound art.

Bomb Dub Mix

Like the EY3 Mix, the remix by DJ Oasis and K Dub Shine utilizes limited material from the original "Banana Chips." It opens with high-hat eighth notes ticking away, accompanied by electric piano and an electric bass laying down a vamp (a short, repeated passage). After eight bars of this vamp, a low-register "Oh yeah" (similar to Yello's famous hit) enters; it is Naoko's "Oh yeah" from the original recording, slowed down. A snare and drone pitch on trumpet adds more timbral layers to the mix. The voice, still slow and low, sings "Ah, banana chips." The DJs apply reverb to both the "ah" and "banana chips," an effect characteristic of dub. The repetition of the vamp and the additive process of layering sounds also give the track a sense of liveness; the feeling is akin to a DJ mixing this for a dancing audience. This transparent compositional process along with the steady groove makes the Bomb Dub Mix more musically accessible than the EY3 Mix. This remix, with its underground chic, hints at a Japanese musical style popular in the 1990s known as Shibuya-kei. Groups like Pizzicato Five and Cornelius popularized this genre, which combines 1960s lounge music, jazz, and soul with techno and J-pop elements.[4] Overall, "Bomb Dub Mix" is a more conventional and cohesive pastiche than the previous remix.

Kenji Sato Mix

The final remix, by Satō Kenji, includes the most musical material from the "Banana Chips" recording. It opens with what sounds like an improvised prelude on electronic synthesizer accompanied by electric bass, electric guitar, and an acoustic stringed instrument. The latter is played in an unconventional percussive style. These instrumental textures provide a foundational repeating sound layer. Like the Bomb Dub Mix, Satō proceeds to compose the remix using an additive process.

The mix samples the chorus and lead vocal tracks from "Banana Chips" in their entirety but adds reverb and lowers their volume relative to the mix. They sound as if the vocals are being played on an old, grainy record. The grain of the recording thus references the tangible musical commodity, the vinyl record, so that the timbre of the vocal tracks link to the history of musical recording and the history of rock, as well as the song's own subliminal commentary on consumerism. Another fascinating component about this remix is that while it sounds the most dance-friendly of the three, it unsettles the tempo and pulse. This sense of displacement is acutely apparent during the chorus of "Banana Chips." The lyric starts on the downbeat (beat one) instead of an upbeat (eighth note before beat four), as it does in the original. As a result, "chips," which was emphasized by falling on a downbeat in the original, appears in a de-emphasized position between the beats in the remix. The rhythmic displacement is slight but unsettling. While the Kenji Sato Mix contains the greatest amount of musical material from the original recording, almost all the original elements are modified. The result is that instead of cutting "Banana Chips" into aural morsels the remix cohesively reworks the single.

Collectively, the three remixes of "Banana Chips" locate the song's aesthetic of repetition and reinterpret it. Additionally, the remixes' deconstructions of the song weaken any sense of a musical climax and endpoint; these remixes could go on forever. They express a need to configure the familiar in new guises and by extension derive new pleasures from them.

Rockin' Bananas: The "Banana Chips" Music Video

While the remixed iterations of "Banana Chips" undermine a female point of enunciation in favor of a DJ's aesthetic, the music video for "Banana Chips" champions it by incorporating elements from Nara Yoshitomo's designs and other components of popular culture, both Japanese and American.

Susan McClary explains the utility of music video analysis:

> Visual images seem to speak much louder than music. . . .Yet it is generally accepted that music in film covertly directs the affective responses of viewers far more than they know. I would suggest that the *music* in music videos is largely responsible for the narrative continuity and affective quality in the resultant work even if it is the visual images we remember concretely. (1991: 161, emphasis in original)

In the "Banana Chips" music video, the music and images inform each other, the colorful computer animation mirroring the song's gleefulness. The video features early animated computer graphic caricatures of the band members Naoko, Atsuko, and Michie as Nara-style dolls; their avatars resemble both the subject on the cover of *Happy Hour* and those in many other works by Nara. Like Nara's female subjects in his paintings and drawings, the girls here are far from helpless; when they can't easily locate their favorite snack, they use superpowers like laser eyes (subtitled "banana chips beam" in the video) to cook up the treat. In their superpowers and general appearance, the Shonen Knife caricatures bear more than a passing resemblance to the Powerpuff Girls (see Image 6.1).

The video follows a loose narrative in which the band searches for banana chips on a tropical island, a supermarket, and a factory. Interspersed between these scenes are shots of the animated women performing the rock song to an audience of dancing bananas.[5] The vignettes take place during the verses while the performance scenes accompany the choruses and guitar solo. Table 6.1 clarifies the video's audiovisual structure.

Image 6.1 *Screen capture from the "Banana Chips" music video. Note that the three members resemble Nara Yoshitomo's doll-like figures.*

Table 6.1 *Chart Outlining Time Codes, Images, and Musical Descriptions for the "Banana Chips" Music Video*

Time Code	Scene Description	Music Description
0:00–0:11	Aerial shot through clouds that zooms in on three doll bodies face down on a sandy beach on a deserted island.	Instrumental Material—hand clapping accompanies overdriven guitar, bass, and drum set cycle through A, D, and E major chords (I, IV, V)
0:12–0:28	The three girls awake on the beach and spot a banana tree. An anthropomorphized banana falls from the tree. A girl zaps him with "banana chips beam." It rains banana chips, which dissolves into the next scene.	Verse 1—consisting of A material (the chords E, A, and E major) and B material (the chords D major, A major, B minor, A, D, A, E, and A major)
0:29–0:42	In an overlapping shot it continues to rain banana chips while the dolls play a rock show for a crowd of dancing bananas. The bass drum features the Shonen Knife logo. The scene ends with an overhead shot of the band. It dissolves to an external overhead shot.	Chorus—"banana chips" consisting of A, D, and E major chords
0:43–0:49	External overhead shot of a map. The camera zooms out from a red building where the show took place and pans left to an orange block and zooms in.	Instrumental Material

(Continued)

Table 6.1 (Continued)

Time Code	Scene Description	Music Description
0:50–0:52	A hard cut to a shot from behind of the three girls riding a scooter.	Instrumental Material continued
0:53–1:09	The girls jump off the scoot and enter a supermarket. Inside the supermarket two girls buy the last bags of banana chips. The last girl must make her own; her friend obliges, using "banana chips beam" from her eyes to make it rain the delicacy. Again there is a dissolve cut of raining chips to the next scene, though it is not overlaid continuously.	Closing of Instrumental Material and Verse 2
1:10–1:21	The band performs for dancing bananas. The section concludes with three compartmentalized shots of the dolls.	Chorus
1:22–1:48	The camera stays in close full shots of the dolls as they play their instruments and the bananas dance. The scene ends again with an overhead shot of the band. It fades to an overhead shot of the red building and a map of the town.	Guitar Solo

Table 6.1 (Continued)

Time Code	Scene Description	Music Description
1:49–1:55	The camera pans down to a set of tan rectangular buildings. It zooms in closer.	Instrumental Material
1:56–2:13	Begins with an establishing shot of a banana chips factory. The girls enter and observe a factory line. One girl works, the other eats banana chips, and the last blasts the bananas with her eye beams. It rains banana chips in a dissolve cut.	Closing of Instrumental Material and Verse 3
2:14–2:28	The band performs for dancing bananas including the anthropomorphized one.	Chorus
2:29–2:39	The band continues playing, but with occasional cross-cuts to a shot of the girls riding a giant banana in the ocean.	Chorus
2:40–2:58	Shot of girls riding the giant banana in the ocean. They are towing a giant bag of banana chips behind them. The scene concludes with a shot of the bag of banana chips on a black background.	Instrumental Material

The music video begins with the animated versions of Naoko, Atsuko, and Michie facedown and shipwrecked on a deserted island. They spot a banana tree and climb up to snag the fruit. Knocking the bushel down, an anthropomorphized banana pops out and Naoko uses her laser eyes to cook up the banana—these are no passive dolls preparing to go hungry on a deserted island! Naoko's laser-beam powers echo those of Tezuka Osamu's famous robot hero Astro Boy (and foreshadow similar powers possessed by the Powerpuff Girls). A shower of banana chips leads into a slow cross-fade. The scene shifts to a performance by the band to an audience filled with faceless dancing bananas as the chorus happily croons "banana chips." Following this, the shot zooms out to reveal a map. It pans to an orange building and then makes a hard cut to a side full shot of the dolls on a scooter, presumably headed to the building, which turns out to be a store specializing in fruit and snacks. Two members snag the last bags of chips (which cost 712 yen) while the third member seems to be left out.[6] Never fear! With an aplomb reminiscent of heroine transformations in anime like *Sailor Moon*, the animated girl summons her superpowers and zaps a regular banana with laser eyes. Banana chips rain down and the video cross-fades back to the performance scene.

Another shot of the map transitions to the final vignette, which takes place at a banana chips factory. The characters work on a conveyor-belt assembly line; one of them munches on the product, conjuring memories of other famous conveyor-belt factory scenes, such as those in Charlie Chaplin's *Modern Times* (1936), *Willy Wonka and the Chocolate Factory* (1971), various scenes from cartoons, and, for American viewers, the famous chocolate factory scene in *I Love Lucy*.[7] In this scene then, Shonen Knife aligns itself with an iconic image of both modernity and popular culture. The scene concludes with the snacking character noticing something peculiar: the banana chips are cooked up not in an oven but with laser-eye beams!

As the chips rain down for the last time, the video cuts to the performance scene for the final, extended chorus. In the outro, the dolls float back to the deserted island on a giant banana with a large bag of banana chips in tow. The final shot depicts a bag of banana chips on a black background.

The music video champions the same atmosphere as Nara's paintings and drawings. The combination of rock and roll with the doll-like Shonen Knife avatars, computer animation, and allusions to magical anime heroines and Lucille Ball makes the cute and cool apparent in the audiovisual medium of the music video. There is a special synergy between image and sound that would not be as effective if the design was by a different artist or the video was shot in live action. The music video, like the remixes, engages with notions of repetition and consumption common to music video aesthetics by replaying the same scenes in conjunction with the chorus and by depicting the Shonen Knife proxies participating in both the creation and consumption of banana chips. This final point matters: just as eating banana chips inspired Naoko to write this song, cultural consumption does not necessarily have to be an end point for late capitalism. The song's guileless music and lyrics, the variety of remixes, and the music video's fusion of Nara's designs with contemporary pop-culture sensibilities illustrate the potential for repetition to symbolize something more than a predetermined matter of course. In "Banana Chips" and its iterations, Shonen Knife shows that ordinary acts of gleeful consumption can be a source of inspiration and creativity.

7 Sweet Candy Power
Shonen Knife's *Josei* Rock Legacy

While Chapter 1 explored the history of female rockers in Japanese music culture up through the 1980s, since then numerous *josei* rock bands have flourished. There is a rich history of *josei* rock in Japan, and Shonen Knife has been a crucial catalyst to the scene's development. Some of the bands discussed in this chapter have strong ties to Shonen Knife and many have found lyrical inspiration in food. There is no way I can address all the *josei* rock groups active today, but I hope this overview encourages others to listen, explore, and research these bands and many others.[1]

The *josei* rock renaissance of the 2000s is multifaceted. Some bands, like Babymetal, are idol concoctions; others, such as Scandal, Tsushimamire, and Noodles, balance sexual appeal with musical creativity. Some stand alone, like the envelope-pushing, noise punk pioneers Otoboke Beaver. KCollectors and Brinky, however, directly draw inspiration from Shonen Knife. All these bands feature female rock musicians front and center, and all these bands exist, in part, thanks to Shonen Knife's trailblazing activities.

Kawaii, Exoticism, and Playing with Stereotypes in *Josei* Rock

Formed in 2010, Babymetal is a corporate-sponsored combination of *kawaii* and hardcore. The brainchild of Kobayashi Kei (nicknamed Kobametal), the original members of Babymetal include Nakamoto Suzuka, Kikuchi Moa, and Mizuno Yui (who went on hiatus in 2018). The trio performs in the typical idol manner, which is characterized by high-pitched vocals and synchronized dance movements. Their vocal harmonies float above a backing band comprised of male instrumentalists performing driving licks and kicking, double-pedal bass drumbeats associated with heavy metal, particularly nu-metal. While the women do not write the music or lyrics, they nonetheless encounter many of the same issues that challenge Shonen Knife and other Japanese female rockers, including stereotypes about Asian women and women in hard rock and heavy metal. In the case of Babymetal, the surprising juxtaposition between the hyper-cute and the hardcore generates a compelling musical combination that has garnered a global fanbase. Kobayashi compared the allure of Babymetal to the ultimate Japanese delicacy, sushi, telling *Metal Hammer* magazine:

> All the old-school metal bands are still around and there's still a fanbase, but it's all getting smaller. So to bring Japanese metal around the world, it has to be something different and original. It's like sushi! Sushi came from Japan and people had never eaten it before, and now everyone eats sushi all over the world. (Begrand 2014)

The comparison between food and music as items of cultural consumption is as applicable to Babymetal as it is to Shonen Knife. Moreover, like Shonen Knife, Babymetal had a hit song inspired by food. "Gimme Chocolate!!" appeared on their self-titled debut album in 2014. Like some of Shonen Knife's tunes, the lyrics of "Gimme Chocolate!!" convey desire for the sweet but also express anxiety about weight gain and body image.[2] Although band manager Kobayashi and Watanabe Miki (who also writes for AKB48) wrote the lyrics, and Ueda Takeshi, bass player and former member of the hardcore band the Mad Capsule Markets, composed the music, I think there is something persuasive about three petite young ladies singing about issues relevant to women. The song, described by Kim Kelly of National Public Radio as "a manic ride through lollipop Hell," opens with thrashing drums, guitar, and electronic zips and zings (Kelly 2018). The verses in the heavier portion of "Gimme Chocolate" are spoke-sung, while the chorus features major-mode harmonies and a tuneful vocal line that intones the lyrics "Check it out, chocolate. Can I have a bit of chocolate? But my weight worries me a bit these days."

In the case of Babymetal, the density of the instrumental textures underscores the femininity of the singers' voices and their voicing of weight anxieties (Plourde 2018: 302). While Shonen Knife's song "I Wanna Eat Chocobars!" relishes the pleasure of eating chocolate, "Gimme Chocolate!!" sweetly and savagely addresses the serious anxieties many women face about body image and food consumption. The tune taps into feelings expressed in Shonen Knife songs like "Diet Run" and "Heavy Song." In this way, Babymetal, similar to Shonen Knife, uses food as a means of grappling with everyday issues many people, whatever their gender, can relate to.

Scandal, akin to Babymetal, also capitalizes on *kawaii* stereotypes in its global promotion. Like Shonen Knife, Scandal's members hail from Osaka. Comprised of Ono Haruna on lead vocals and rhythm guitar, Sasazaki Mami on lead guitar, Ogawa Tomomi on bass, and Suzuki Rina on drums and keyboard, the band formed in 2006. In the past decade, the band has found growing popularity both at home and abroad thanks to popular anime shows like *Bleach* and *Fullmetal Alchemist: Brotherhood* featuring Scandal's music. Like Shonen Knife, Scandal too have nurtured a cross-pollination between cartoon shows and rock music; they even made music videos featuring anime versions of themselves. The band has performed at anime conventions, as well as festivals like the annual South by Southwest (SXSW) in Austin, Texas.

All of Scandal's nine albums have charted in the top five, solidifying their position as the *josei* rock band with the most best-selling albums. Their 2018 album, *Honey*, reached number three on the Japanese Oricon music chart. While *Honey* does not feature any food-related songs, the title plays with the multiple meanings of the word. First, while English is not uncommon, it is notable that Scandal decided to use the English word "honey" instead of the Japanese word *hachimitsu*. This indicates Scandal's desire to appeal to a cool, bilingual group of local listeners and pursue an outward address to a global community of fans. The word itself refers to the food, sweet and syrupy, a delectable realization of *kawaii* in edible form, as well as an affectionate and sometimes unwanted nickname applied to young women. The album title also hints at the source of honey production, the fuzzy bumble bee that visits flowers but also wields a wicked stinger when threatened. In this, the bee functions as a metaphor for the *josei* rockers; they may look cute, they may produce sweet products, but they are not helpless. Scandal expresses multiple nuances related to being Japanese female rock musicians on an international stage.

Significantly, Scandal also writes most of their music and lyrics; in late 2018, its members established their own record label called "her" (Bolan 2018). As a band, Scandal has navigated a path as hard-hitting, accomplished female rockers within the broader realm of Japanese popular culture. Their connection to anime, as well as their willingness to don sexy-cute outfits, has certainly helped their music, which ranges from pop punk and funk to heavier fare, rise to the top of the charts. The leaning into stereotypes as a means of reclaiming agency is a practice common in many *josei* rock groups ranging from the mainstream to the underground. Each band takes up the challenge of appropriating, dismantling, and playing with these global stereotypes, so much so that the practice is woven into the aesthetic fabric of *josei* rock.

While Babymetal and Scandal represent *josei* rock in mainstream Japanese music culture, several other bands of note thrive on the indie circuit. Many of these groups have some connection to Shonen Knife, playing live shows with the veteran band and drawing inspiration from them. Tsushimamire is one such *josei* rock group.[3] Self-described as an "art punk rock trio from Tokyo, Japan," Tsushimamire is a three-piece group that has performed with Shonen Knife and was briefly on the same American record distributor, Good Charamel Records. Kono Mari (lead vocals and guitar), Tsushima Yayoi (bass guitar), and Masuda Mizue (drums) formed the band in 1999, when they met in college. Masuda departed the band in 2017 and was replaced by current drummer Takagi Maiko. Like Shonen Knife, Tsushimamire's songs cut across genre boundaries; their tunes include elements of punk, pop, heavy rock, and even rap. They have also written several songs about food, including "Tea Time Ska," "Brain Shortcake" (Nō Miso Shortcake), "Fish Cakes" (Kamaboko), and "American Hamburger." This last track appeared on their first single, "Hamburger Set," released in 1999. As such, it reveals a taste not only for the United States delicacy but also for hooks, hard rock, and raw, tuneful vocals. The sound recalls early Shonen Knife. Similar to Shonen Knife, Tsushimamire recorded a song for the Japanese release of *The Powerpuff Girls* cartoon. In an interview, they related the story behind recording "Hyper Sweet Power": "When we watched PPG, we fell in love with PPG. They are so cute, tough and rock like us!!! So we decided to make new songs for PPG. We tried to make this song which makes everybody feel happy" (Smith 2010).

Tsushimamire's attitude is the same as Shonen Knife's—both bands want to make songs that make people feel happy, and both felt some affinity for the superhero sisters. The song "Hyper Sweet Power" balances cute with the cool. It is significantly heavier and features more distortion than Shonen Knife's "Buttercup (I'm a Super Girl)." But akin to their predecessors, Tsushimamire uses tight vocal harmonies and a combination of English and Japanese in the tune. Given the many similarities between Tsushimamire and Shonen Knife, it is no surprise that they have performed together at numerous venues across Japan.

Noodles, active since 1991, also has some clear connections to Shonen Knife. Based out of Yokohama, near Tokyo, Noodles is a power trio comprised of Yoko (vocals/guitar), Ikuno (bass guitar), and Ayumi (drums) (Robson 2010).[4] The band's name is of course a food reference; like Scandal's *Honey*, the word "noodles" too conveys multiple meanings simultaneously. Noodles is obviously an English word (*men* is the typical word for noodles in Japanese); as such, the band's name expresses an internationality. The band sings in both English and Japanese, and by 2004, Noodles had begun touring in the United States and playing SXSW. Their sound is garage rock grunge with a feminine flare; they cited the Breeders as one of their main influences, and even opened for them at the Breeder's 2003 show in Osaka (Robson 2010).

Noodles also has some close ties to Shonen Knife. They regularly play shows together and both appeared on the lineup for Nara Yoshitomo's sixtieth birthday party in 2019. Just as he did the album art for *Happy Hour* in 1998, Nara also created the album art for Noodles' 2019 album *I'm Not Chic*. Like *Happy Hour*, this artwork features the large-eyed doll figures Nara is known for. In the case of *I'm Not Chic*'s album art, the figure is not overly cute. The girl with jagged hair and a T-shirt does not smile; the angle of her pencil-line lips is one of defiance. Noodles also has a few songs with food in the titles, though they rarely deal with food consumption. Examples of these include "Cinnamon Tambourine," "Sugar Drum," "Summer Coffee," "Silent Apple," and "Grapefruit Juice." The latter of these tunes encapsulates the band's sound. Appearing on the compilation album *Life Is Delicious*, it is a relaxed garage rock song reminiscent of tunes from Radiohead's *Pablo Honey*. Noodles' members typically wear jeans and T-shirts for shows, clinching their rejection of *kawaii* in favor of the cool both in image and in music. This cool introspection on the part of this *josei* rock trio provides a counterbalance to overwhelmingly more common *kawaii* approach. Noodles quite simply doesn't seem to give a fuck about stereotypes and expectations. And what, in the end, is more punk than that?

The answer might be Otoboke Beaver. A quartet from Kyoto, Otoboke Beaver's music hovers in the nebulous space between hardcore punk rock and noise music. Their frank, in-your-face performance style and lyrics that mix local slang with English are especially refreshing. Formed in 2009, they are among the most recent *josei* rock bands to emerge on the international scene. Comprised of Accorinrin on main vocals, Yoyoyoshie on guitar, Hiro-chan on bass, and Kahokiss (who replaced original drummer Pop in July of 2018), the members met at Kyoto's Ritsumeikan University student music club, which happened to be the same one former Shonen Knife member Morimoto Emi participated in years earlier. Playing local gigs at first, Otoboke Beaver broke into the U.S. scene in the late 2010s, performing at Coachella in 2018 and SXSW in 2019. That same year they also released a compilation album of new and previously distributed material called *Itekoma Hits* and appeared on a double bill with Shonen Knife in Osaka in December. In early 2020, the members of Otoboke Beaver quit their day jobs and planned to embark on their "Yametatta Tour" of Europe (*yametatta* is Kyoto dialect for "having recently quit"). They released an accompanying single, "Dirty Old Fart Is Waiting for My Reaction," which critiques misogynist comments posted about the band on social media.

Like seasoned bands such as Shonen Knife and the 5678s, Otoboke Beaver's members frequently perform in 1960s-style dresses. They occasionally incorporate idol-esque dance moves.[5] Otoboke Beaver's music, however, is much more aggressive than Shonen Knife's. The feminine retro outfits and girlish dance moves contrast with the overdriven guitars, raucous drums, and screaming vocals that characterize Otoboke Beaver's music. In this way, the band brilliantly plays with the concept of *kawaii*, transforming cuteness into a postmodern avant-garde aesthetic that rejects stereotypes. If at times Shonen Knife's performance of femininity is tongue-in-cheek, then Otoboke Beaver's approach is downright dark. The band name, for example, seems to be a cute animal reference; "otoboke beaver" literally means "beaver feigning ignorance/playing dumb." But the phrase has a specifically sexual connotation to it as well. The band named themselves after a love hotel in Osaka, and in the English language, beaver is a euphemism for female genitalia (Jagota 2019). The women of Otoboke Beaver, in other words, are not afraid to assert their sexuality and desires via their musical output. On occasion, the lyrical topic of food serves as a vehicle for this assertion.[6]

"After Making Love With Me, You Eat Your Wife's Meal!" (Anata watashi daita ato yome no meshi), a 2018 single and 2019 music video, serves as an exemplar of Otoboke Beaver's defiance.[7] The title alludes to an extramarital relationship. In the span of around two minutes, the singing character undergoes a cathartic transformation: at first, she is furious with her lover for returning home to eat his wife's cooking, then she realizes she herself is being used, and finally she rejects the lover with a firm, "Don't make a meal of me—I say NO!" Food imagery appears throughout the song in connection to female sexuality; *dashi,* or fish broth, becomes a metaphor for either tears or female ejaculate, and *shibazuke,* which are Kyoto-style *shiso* pickles that are a pinkish-purple hue, allude to genitalia. *Shibazuke* becomes part of a ritualistic chant embedded in the song: "sex, *shibazuke,* rock and roll!" sing the women as they clap hands. The chant is a play on the phrase "sex, drugs, and rock and roll." By incorporating and modifying this rock cliché, the members of Otoboke Beaver disassemble (Western, male) rock history and transform it into something Japanese, female, and radically punk.

Otoboke Beaver's approach to food in this song is drastically different from Shonen Knife's. Whereas in Shonen Knife, food itself is a source of desire, pleasure, and sometimes anxiety, for Otoboke Beaver food is a polysemic symbol not only of sexual desire but also of a reclamation of self and rejection of societal norms. The song's accompanying music video clarifies this interpretation. Like the song itself, which alternates between screaming vocals and hardcore punk accompaniment with more restrained, repetitive chants, the video too juxtaposes the sweet with the grotesque. It begins with the four band members wearing Western-style bridal dresses. White sheets drape the walls behind them. The music video soon descends into the absurd. First, Yoyoyoshie pan-fries a bridal bouquet. Then each member presents the camera (representing the male gaze) with a homemade dish—spaghetti and meatballs, *onigiri* (Japanese rice balls), curry, and *takoyaki* (an Osaka delicacy of fried dough balls with octopus).[8] The brides fall into violent food fight. They grapple with each other, smearing food, and Accorinrin, in a masculine gesture, bites a huge chunk of meat off a skewer.

A momentary pause from the intense music and visuals occurs in synchronization with the repeated line in English: "jealousy in my dust box." Accorinrin carefully balances a wedding cake on a large shovel, an image that conjures a similarly ridiculous food-rock moment: the scene from the Beatles' film *Magical Mystery Tour* (1967) in which John Lennon shovels mounds of spaghetti onto a diner's plate. Both the Beatles' and Otoboke Beaver's imagery are absurdist commentaries on consumption. Otoboke Beaver's music video directly addresses gender roles, particularly the role the wife is expected to fulfill in society as a creator and provider of meals. The scene concludes with the bride throwing the cake at the camera; the cake's destruction simultaneously rejects the female as a sweet and delicately decorated object, as well as the rituals of matrimony and married life.

The second half of the video becomes even more surreal. The filthy brides punch an inflated, man-shaped bag, stir empty pots, serve up a sponge, weigh a heart, and eat long black hair from a ramen bowl. A marriage registration form is torn in half. After another musical respite, the "sex, *shibazuke*, rock and roll" chant accompanies the brides lining up, smiling and waving their arms side to side in a synchronized dance that recalls the cute choreographed movements of idol stars. A throaty scream and blazing instrumental breakdown obliterate the moment into a wall of noise. As Accorinrin intones the concluding line "make a meal out of me," the women appear covered in half-off stickers commonly seen on boxes of prepared food at supermarkets toward closing time. The stickers on the women's bodies are reflecting on societal concepts of what it means to be out-of-date, reaching limits on "freshness" (i.e., marriageable age), before being thrown out with the garbage. The video concludes with the four members sitting in traditional *seiza* style with legs tidily tucked underneath their sit bones and bowing to the camera, a submissive action brides perform at traditional Japanese wedding ceremonies. Behind them the food-stained walls sport a graffiti heart (Image 7.1).

However, the video is not over. In a postlude, the women dance around a pagan-esque bonfire, singing and clapping "sex, *shibazuke*, rock and roll." On closer inspection, the effigy in the center of the fire is revealed to be the four wedding dresses. This final shot cements the political commentary at the core of "After Making Love With Me, You Eat Your Wife's Meal!": marriage and the historical gender roles it entails are turned to ashes. I have

Image 7.1 *Screen capture from "After Making Love With Me, You Eat Your Wife's Meal!" music video by Otoboke Beaver. The four brides, filthy from their food fight, ironically bow to the camera's male gaze.*

Image 7.2 *Screen capture from the postlude to "After Making Love With Me, You Eat Your Wife's Meal!" music video by Otoboke Beaver. The women dance around a bonfire of burning wedding dresses chanting "sex, shibazuke, rock and roll!"*

spent a significant amount of space analyzing Otoboke Beaver's song and music video because while they, like Shonen Knife, draw on food for lyrical inspiration, they do so in a very different way. The younger group engages with food and music as a means of exploring social issues and infuses their output with raw political critiques characteristic of punk. As inheritors to Shonen Knife's legacy, Otoboke Beaver are bravely creative, unapologetically abrasive, and completely cool (Image 7.2).

Cover Bands and Inspired Homages

Two other bands have direct ties to Shonen Knife in terms of inspiration and musical performance. I had the chance to meet with members of the KCollectors and Brinky and chat with them about Shonen Knife and food.[9] The KCollectors are a trio of women—Kyoko (vocals and guitar), Tama-chan (bass), and Mamiko (drums)—who perform shows as a Shonen Knife cover band. They are longtime fans and friends of Shonen Knife—*The Shonen Knife Nexus* publisher George Handlon dubbed Mamiko Shonen Knife's number one fan. The KCollectors, who originally played together under the name Giant Kitty, have been active as a cover group since 2014. They perform regularly in the Tokyo area, where they are based. When I asked them about the role of female rockers in Japan, they mentioned the huge influence Princess Princess had on girls in the 1980s. As the first *josei* rock band to perform at the Tokyo Budōkan, Princess Princess showed that it was possible for Japanese women to achieve success in rock and roll (Chapter 1). This kind of visibility and representation in media played a crucial role in inspiring young women in the 1980s and up through to today. However, Mamiko pointed out, Princess Princess and many other massively successful *josei* bands from that era are now defunct; in this regard, Shonen Knife is a special anomaly (KCollectors, interview with the author, December 18, 2018, Tokyo).

Mamiko suggested that the release of *Let's Knife* in 1992 was a turning point for Shonen Knife. Thanks to that album, the band received more attention on the Japanese scene. Kyoko and Mamiko suggested that part of this might have had to do with the group's improved instrumental abilities. Nevertheless, from KCollectors' point of view, the band always had a special knack for writing catchy songs. "Once we hear them, we will never forget (them)," Mamiko related (KCollectors, interview). Shonen Knife's earworm charm is thanks to their "simple but cool" music, as Kyoko puts it (KCollectors, interview).[10] KCollectors' own set list typically includes a few songs about food, and they have performed "Banana Chips," "Ramen Rock," and "Sweet Candy Power." Interestingly, when a given song has both a Japanese and an English version, Kyoko usually prefers to sing in English, which she and Mamiko both speak excellently. Kyoko admitted singing in English is easier in some ways; if she makes a mistake with the lyrics, no one really notices. Explaining Shonen Knife's penchant for food songs, Mamiko believed that the band prefers to write about things they like and know, rather than writing about broken hearts: "everybody is interested in food," she said (KCollectors, interview).

Certainly, the Kawano family would agree with this statement. Brinky is a family band; mother Kawano Maki manages the band, father Kenji plays bass, their elder daughter Risa plays drums, and their younger daughter Rina sings and plays guitar.[11] They started playing together in April of 2011, when Risa was sixteen and Rina was only eleven years old; a month later, Rina had turned twelve and Brinky played their first live show. Shonen Knife had a huge impact on Brinky since its inception. At their first show, Brinky covered several Shonen Knife songs, including "Twist Barbie," "Riding on the Rocket," and "Banana Chips." When the family finally had a chance to see Shonen Knife perform live in 2012 at the 712 show at Osaka's live house Pangea, they were struck by the straightforward music and the fun atmosphere. This is something worth lingering on; at shows, Shonen Knife smiles almost the whole time, as do many audience members. The Shonen Knife live show experience is vastly different from typical punk shows in the United States; there is no rage or violent thrashing.[12] Brinky members noted that songs about food contribute to the show's pleasant vibes. Food, they related, makes a great lyrical topic because it's easier to write songs about things you like (Brinky, personal email communication, June 22, 2019).

As a result, Brinky too has written several original songs about food, including ones about pudding, cheese, chicken nuggets, bread, sweet red bean and butter sandwiches, shortbread, and donuts. "Hot Donuts" is an excellent example of Brinky's energetic punk sound inspired by Shonen Knife. Around two minutes long, the tune opens with an overdriven guitar hook; soon bass and drums join in a thumping good time. The lyrics, written by Michael Stephens and performed in English by Rina, describe late-night donut cravings and acquiring a dozen hot donuts. Two verses precede a chorus of "I need some donuts NOW!" A third verse references the donut-loving cartoon character Homer Simpson before the final chorus catapults the song to its joyous conclusion. The blazing, happy heaviness of the tune sounds like some of the 1970s rock-inspired songs by Shonen Knife. Of course, this is thanks in part to Brinky's Risa joining Shonen Knife on the drums in 2015. Since that time, Risa has rocked on the Shonen Knife albums *Adventure* (2016), *ALIVE! In Osaka* (2018), and *Sweet Candy Power* (2019). On the former two albums, she sings the Naoko-penned tune "Green Tangerine." The song is a tuneful ode to the *kabosu,* a citrus fruit associated with the northern Kyushu prefecture of Ōita and used to flavor a variety of Japanese dishes. Risa, like the other members of Shonen Knife, is a devoted foodie and enjoys tasting a variety of cuisines while on tour abroad. Fittingly, on *Sweet Candy Power*, she provides lead vocals on one of the two tracks about food: "Ice Cream Cookie Sandwiches."

Strong and Sweet

Since the release of *Happy Hour* in 1998, Shonen Knife has maintained a devotion to food with songs like "Rock 'n' Roll Cake" (*Free Time,* 2010), "Fortune Cookie" (*Overdrive,* 2014), "Wasabi" (*Adventure,* 2016), and on *Sweet Candy Power*, "Ice Cream Cookie Sandwiches" and "Sweet Candy Power." Like the songs of the prior decades, these two tracks illustrate an unwavering devotion to food as a source of creativity and as a means of subtly engaging with gender. The album title *Sweet Candy Power* perfectly captures the band's duality; the members are both sweet and strong, *kawaii* and cool.

"Ice Cream Cookie Sandwiches" is a delectable ode to the dessert. It is an upbeat, major-mode number with a straightforward structure of an instrumental opening followed by a verse and chorus that is then repeated. But within the uncomplicated musical components are some nuances. For example, both verses contrast the competing desserts of ice cream and cookies. In the opening verse's lines, "I like cookies" and "I like ice cream," the vocals are in unison. Upon entering the pre-chorus on the line, "You ask me which do I like better," the vocals break into three-part harmony. This could be written off as simply neat part-writing, but closer examination encourages listeners to consider the symbolic quality of the harmonic texture. Instead of just one voice trying to choose between one dessert, there are now three vocal lines singing in harmony. They metaphorically represent a sugary trinity: the cookie, the ice cream, and the ideal union of the two in the ice cream cookie sandwich. This harmonic layering foreshadows the solution of the ice cream cookie sandwich crooned about in the chorus. As Risa sings "ice cream cookies," a chorus echoes her, and in the final line of the chorus, the vocals again split into harmonies on "ice cream cookie sandwiches are the best way to eat." The vocal harmony musically portrays the delectable harmony between cookie and ice cream.

Naoko sings the album's title track "Sweet Candy Power." Like "Ice Cream Cookie Sandwiches," this song too contains some delicate twists and turns beneath its unassuming façade. Changes in the musical material are densely packed throughout the approximately three-minute song. The structure of "Sweet Candy Power" can be broken into four sections which then repeat. The opening is similar to "BBQ Party" in that it begins slowly with only vocals and guitar. Naoko sings about the many joys of candy. This prelude dangles on a V chord and buzzing feedback enters the mix; drumsticks hammer out a new tempo. The tune shifts from pop rock sweetness to hardcore in a blink. *Amai* (written in Roman alphabet as "am I" in the lyrics sheet) is intoned four times in a short-long pattern that places the syllables on different beats with each iteration. A hardcore punk shout of "candy" follows the iterations. This line alone is intriguing for its wordplay. In the album's accompanying booklet, the lyrics are written "am I," implying that the singer is wondering if she is candy. Is she becoming what she eats? Or is this another metaphor? Is the singer candy-like, sweet but hard? Yet, if one simply listens to the lyrics, it is easy to assume she is singing *amai*, the Japanese word for "sweet."

The music video of "Sweet Candy Power" clarifies the wordplay between *amai* and "am I." In the opening Naoko plays guitar and sings in front of a wall covered in drawings of fashionable young women. At the transitional *amai*, each iteration of the phrase features a band member—in addition to Atsuko and Risa, Naru and Ritsuko, who still sometimes play at shows and record with the group. Overlaid on these shots are "Am I" in Roman alphabet and *amai* in *katakana, hiragana* (the Japanese syllabic scripts), and *kanji* (the Chinese character for the word). The result is that the music video, like so much of Shonen Knife, gestures toward a transnational flow of language, music, and of course sweets.

However, the band never relinquishes their Osaka roots. During the chorus, Osaka landmarks like *Taiyō no tō* (the

Image 7.3 *Screen capture from the "Sweet Candy Power" music video by Shonen Knife. Naoko enjoys an oversized peppermint candy at Dōtonbori, a famous Osaka district.*

Tower of the Sun, erected for the 1970 World Expo) and Osaka Castle appear in the background of shots. In the next verse, Naoko appears in multiple shots wearing various rock band T-shirts. Cherry blossoms, Osaka's Umeda train station, and the Dōtonbori district appear behind her. With its visual references to the Yamanos' hometown that is famous for "eating 'til you drop" (*kuidaore*), the video captures Shonen Knife's career as food-loving musicians bridging the local and the cosmopolitan, as well as the cute and the cool (Image 7.3).

Gochisōsama Deshita (That Was a Delicious Meal!)

The food-related tracks on *Sweet Candy Power* represent a common theme throughout Shonen Knife's extended career. "Ice Cream Cookie Sandwiches" and "Sweet Candy Power" are memorable, happy songs, but behind their ingenuous sound are some fascinating musical details. The interplay between music and text in these and many other tunes shows that Shonen Knife is a multivalent group of musicians; they are not just another girl group, nor do they cater to *kawaii* exoticism or limit themselves to preconceived ideas about punk, pop, rock, or any other genre. They are singular, sweet, strong, creative artists who have influenced and inspired multiple generations of female rock musicians and will likely continue to do so for years to come (Image 7.4).

Since the early 1980s and up through the present day, food plays a major role in their creative output. A single glance at Shonen Knife's tour blog and social media sites instantly

Image 7.4 *Shonen Knife rocks out at a show in Denver, Colorado during their Sweet Candy Power Tour. Left to right: Kawano Risa, Yamano Atsuko, Yamano Naoko. Taken September 3, 2019. Photo courtesy of Shannon Bailey.*

broadcasts the band's love for food. The women are conscious of the central role food plays in both their music and their relationship with fans. Pictures of delicious dishes, some homemade and some store-bought, saturate their social media updates. Food is also a crucial part of their live performances. For example, at the 712 shows in 2018 Shonen Knife played a mini-set comprised entirely of food songs. Naoko even joked afterward, "Now we are all full!" Additionally, Shonen Knife's performance banter commonly includes a story about something they recently ate while on tour. On the single "Better," released online during the COVID-19 pandemic, Naoko encourages listeners to be optimistic, and, in the meantime, eat delicious ice cream among other things.[13] In short, Shonen

Knife recognizes the appeal of food as a universal "happy object" that can cheer global audiences. As Naoko told National Public Radio in a 2017 interview, "I found that eating delicious food is the most important thing for people," she says. "It's a kind of universal topic" (Godoy 2017). By fusing lyrics about food with the accessible sounds of pop punk, Shonen Knife conveys an optimistic message of locating happiness in the everyday that delights listeners around the world. Celebrity chef and food critic Anthony Bourdain declared, "food may not be the answer to world peace, but it's a start."[14] Through decades of recordings and musical activities, Shonen Knife has shown that food and music, while not answers, are valuable starting points for understanding people and their cultures.

Throughout this book, I have argued that food is a pillar in Shonen Knife's music; symbolically, food alludes to traditional notions of women preparing food for families and by extension showing love through food, as exemplified by carefully crafted lunchboxes with cute Pikachu-shaped pickles or Totoro-whiskered rice balls in Japan, or by tables heaving under the weight of heaping mounds of potato salad, biscuits, ham, and cakes in Oklahoma. But beyond being a product of unpaid female labor, food can also represent liberation, especially when it comes to taking pleasure in consuming delicacies without guilt or worry. Like the heroine Mikage in Yoshimoto Banana's novel *Kitchen*, Shonen Knife treats food as a means to self-empowerment and connection with others. The central theme of food in their oeuvre encompasses the domestic and public roles women perform in society as wives, mothers, friends, workers, and even rock stars. Shonen Knife uses a "feminine" topic like food and combines it with a

Image 7.5 *Shonen Knife wraps up a hard-rocking live show in Denver, Colorado, during their Sweet Candy Power Tour. Left to right: Yamano Atsuko, Kawano Risa, Yamano Naoko. Photo courtesy of Shannon Bailey.*

variety of musical genres, including punk and hard rock, to create a sound that challenges stereotypes about Japanese women, cuteness, and coolness. This blending brings to mind the opening credits of each *Powerpuff Girls* episode, which explain that the super heroines are made of "sugar, spice, and everything nice," like the old adage says, but along with the mysterious ingredient, Chemical X. In their persistence, performance, and extensive musical output, Shonen Knife, like the Powerpuff Girls, proves that femininity and strength are not mutually exclusive (Image 7.5).

Notes

Introduction

1 Shonen Knife has a long connection with the Ramones. They opened for the Ramones on their farewell tour of Japan in 1996, recorded a cover album called *Osaka Ramones* (2011), and toured with C. J. Ramone.

2 Atsuko related that she practiced on phone books via Twitter. See @SK_Atsuko, December 29, 2018.

3 Their first show took place at Osaka Studio One. About thirty-six people attended, paying the cover price of 100 yen (around one dollar). See "Shonen Knife Biography," accessed February 16, 2020, http://www.shonenknife.net/bios/bios1982.html.

4 Sub Pop later released Shonen Knife's single "Neon Zebra" in 1991.

5 Shonen Knife's cover of Weird Al Yankovic's "Eat It," a parody of Michael Jackson's "Beat It," supremely exemplifies this complexity. See *Dr. Demento Covered in Punk* (2018).

6 Sullivan (2001) cites Naoko's eschewing of the political. Several philosophers, most notably those of the Frankfurt School, have argued that mass culture is not apolitical. See Horkheimer and Adorno (2002).

7 To this point, Naoko cites "Black Bass" as being a song about environmental issues.

Chapter 1

1 For more on Sakamoto and Elvis, see Bourdaghs (2012: 97–101).

2 Like Hibari, Eri Chiemi had a solo career that took her to the United States for concert tours. While there she reportedly hoped to take singing lessons from Kaye Starr, Rosemary Clooney, and Ella Fitzgerald (Bourdaghs 2012: 59).

3 Branstetter is a musicologist as well as the digital education manager at the Rock & Roll Hall of Fame in Cleveland, Ohio. Her 2019 online project, *Women in Rock & Roll's First Wave*, was created in partial fulfillment of her dissertation project at Case Western University.

4 In recent years, female Beatles cover bands have appeared in Japan, most notably the Clover. Mamiko of KCollectors also performs in a Beatles cover band. For more on the KCollectors and Mamiko, see Chapter 7.

5 The title, "Sōran-bushi a go-go," references the popular folk song, "Sōran Bushi," believed to have originated in Japan's northernmost island Hokkaido as a fishermen's tune. In the modern era, the song became popular across the country, thanks to its appearance at school functions like annual sports days (*undōkai*). Students frequently perform a dance along with the song that is associated with Obon, a festival that honors the spirits of the dead.

6 Later *josei* bands like Shonen Knife, the 5678s, and Otoboke Beaver have embraced 1960s-style dresses as stage costumes. Naoko related that Shonen Knife's outfits are a nod to the Supremes and the Ronettes (Yamano N., personal communication, Aug. 10, 2020).

7. There are several *josei* rock bands of this time period that I have not discussed in this book, including the 5678s, Zelda, Mescaline Drive, Papaya Paranoia, Go-Bangs, and Sekiri (Dysentery). The former is perhaps best known in the United States thanks to their appearance in Quentin Tarantino's *Kill Bill Vol. 1* (2003).
8. Shonen Knife also recorded a cover of "Cherry Bomb" in English. It appears on *Pretty Little Baka Guy* (1986).
9. Biography, Tenko Official Site.
10. Biography, Show-ya Official Site.
11. For more on the idol system and AKB48, see Galbraith and Karlin (2019).
12. Okui Kaori changed her surname to Kishitani after her marriage to Kishitani Gorō.
13. While Shonen Knife has not yet played at the Budōkan, Atsuko has performed there. She reportedly sang backing vocals at Cheap Trick's performance at the Budōkan in 1978. See Hensley (1997).

Chapter 2

1. The original lineup of Yamano Naoko, Yamano Atsuko, and Nakatani Michie remained intact until 1999. That year, Michie retired from the band and Atsuko switched from drums to bass guitar and played with the band in that capacity until 2006. Atsuko went on hiatus from 2006–2015. Since 2015, she has been an active part of the lineup, frequently joining on bass for North American shows since and occasionally for other shows as well. Drummers

Nishiura Mana (touring drummer, 2001–4), Nakanishi Etsuko (official member, 2005–2010), and Morimoto Emi (official member, 2010–15) played with the band until Kawano Risa joined (official member, 2015–present). Risa has since been a regular in the lineup. Bassists Taneda Ritsuko (official member, 2006–present, on hiatus 2015–17) and Ishizuka Naru (official member, 2015–present) sometimes perform with the band or help in other capacities.

2 Shonen Knife also has written several songs about animals, another "happy object" (unless of course the animal is the vicious dog referenced in "Dogfight").

3 Some songs are not included though they reference eating at one point, such as "Elephant Pao Pao," "Black Bass," and "Monster Jellyfish." Some songs like "Banana Leaf" and "Banana Fish" contain food in their titles but are not about eating, so they are not included in the table. I included "Deer Biscuits" because it is about food and feeding the eponymous animal.

4 Food can, of course, serve as a metaphor for sexual desire, as it does in literature and music as wide-ranging as Henry Fielding's *Tom Jones*, Laura Esquivel's *Like Water for Chocolate* to Warrant's "Cherry Pie" and Nicki Minaj's "Ice Cream Man." The Japanese film director Itami Jūzō also emphasized the connection between food and sex in his 1985 film *Tampopo*. Shonen Knife's food songs, though, do not hint toward this trope so baldly.

5 For a discussion on global pop and authenticity, see Taylor (1997: 21–31).

6 The word "*kawaii*," translated as "lovely" in this case, is also commonly translated as "cute."

Chapter 3

1. The song "Dizzy" from *Sweet Candy Power* (2019) briefly mentions dieting as a possible cause of dizziness.

2. Consciousness about food and weight gain is apparent in Japanese popular culture and even manifested at the 712 Shonen Knife show on July 7, 2018. Naoko teased Risa about enjoying too many shortbread cookies during their European tour.

3. "Cannibal Papaya" also appears remixed by Thurston Moore on *Super Mix* (1997). The title's translation as "Cannibal Papaya" is somewhat confusing since the papaya monster consumes human beings, not other papayas.

4. For example, the *Godzilla* film series frequently depicts South Pacific islanders as primitive Others living in harmony with nature. For more on this, see Rhoads and McCorkle (2018: 56–8, 67–8).

5. I discuss the peccadillos of recording songs in dual languages in greater detail in Chapter 5.

6. Another track on *Rock Animals*, "Cobra vs Mongoose" is also a heavy grunge rock track. This track was voted as a fan favorite rarity that was performed at the 712 shows in July of 2018.

7. Two lines in particular stick out in the Japanese lyrics: "Red beverage tomato juice, always healthy in my life" (*akai nomimono tomato jūsu, itsmo herushī in mai raifu*) and "Put in some lemon juice and (I) always feel like dynamite" (*remon no shiru o tarashite kibun ha itsumo dainamaito*). Both convey the healthy benefits of citrus.

8. The first document to refer to chocolate in Japan was that of a prostitute who visited the Dutch trading post. In

her records, she reported receiving a tip of six chocolates (Chocolate and Cocoa Association of Japan).

9 Meter refers to the number of beats in a given unit of musical time (measure). Most Shonen Knife songs are in 4/4 time, with four beats per measure.

10 Marcel Proust eloquently depicts the powerful relationship between food and memory in *In Search of Lost Time: Time Regained* (Proust 2003).

11 This reference to picnicking under a cherry tree alludes to the Japanese tradition of *hanami,* or cherry blossom viewing. Parties for viewing cherry blossoms, held since the eighth century, usher in the spring. Cherry blossoms are also commonly featured in poetry, as the transitory nature of the *hanami* season captures the pathos of the ever-changing nature of existence.

12 A similar effect is built into the track "Dizzy" (2019) from *Sweet Candy Power*. In this song, the band guides the audience in a stomping and clapping rhythm reminiscent of Queen's "We Will Rock You."

Chapter 4

1 The complete track listing for the American release included "Shonen Knife Planet," "Konnichiwa," "Cookie Day," "Hot Chocolate," "Sushi Bar Song," "Fish Eyes," "Banana Chips," "Dolly," "Jackalope," "Gyoza," "Catch Your Bus," "People Traps," "His Pet," and "Daydream Believer."

2 The band discussed their excitement about collaborating with Microsoft in an interview with *Weekly Ascii*. In it, they looked forward to meeting Bill Gates and sharing music with the entire web community. Their relationship with Microsoft dated to a few years earlier, when the company used Shonen Knife's cover of the Carpenters'"Top of the World" for a Windows 95 commercial. See Tanaka (1998).

3 See Asia Society, *Yoshitomo Nara Nobody's Fool*.

Chapter 5

1 For more on Hawaiian cuisine, see Lauden (1996).

2 In the immediate postwar years, the United States in particular contributed to transforming the Japanese diet by selling flour and powdered milk to Japan and encouraging bread and milk to be served with school lunches. See Sheng (2017: 208).

3 Kitagawa Junko notes that in 2012, female teachers made up 62.7 percent of elementary school teachers in Japan, though in middle and high schools, male teachers comprise the majority (Kitagawa 2013: 50). In elementary school, then, women frequently fulfill the role of both educator and surrogate mother, just as they do at preschools and daycares. Elementary school students are taught the importance of eating healthy, well-balanced meals, and everyone, teachers and students alike, eat the same school lunch (*kyūshoku*).

4 "Good wives, wise mothers" was a propaganda slogan popular in the late nineteenth and early twentieth centuries to encourage women to contribute to Japan's national well-being. However, while the actual imperialistic words are rarely invoked today, the concept conveyed by the slogan remains prominent.

5 One exception to this is Chidui Yuki, who opened her restaurant Nadeshico Sushi in Tokyo in 2010.

6 Naoko mentioned that the band returned to the same sushi bar years later and it was still tasty—and still serving miso soup before the meal (Yamano N., interview).

7 An earlier Shonen Knife tune, "Chinese Song" (appearing on *Yama No Attchan*), incorporates similar musical components, including upper-register bells and a gong.

8 Edgar W. Pope has documented a history of Japanese popular musicians incorporating Orientalists tropes into their performances in the early twentieth century. See Pope (1993).

9 Bourdaghs relates that another influential Japanese band, Yellow Magic Orchestra, enacted a similar appropriation of self-Orientalist tropes a generation earlier. See Bourdaghs (2012: 186–92). Shuhei Hosokawa has also addressed self-Orientalism in the music of Yellow Magic Orchestra. See Hosokawa (1999). Interestingly, there is a connection between YMO and Shonen Knife. YMO band member and composer Sakamoto Ryūichi remixed the Shonen Knife tune "Insect Collector." This remix appeared on a collection of Shonen Knife songs called *Super Mix* (1997).

10 "Hot Chocolate" originally appeared on the mini-album *It's a New Find* (1997) and a remix of it by Stereolab is included on *Ultra Mix* (1997).

Chapter 6

1 If one wanted to perform a Freudian interpretation of "Banana Chips" it would certainly be possible. That, however, is beyond the purview of this book.

2 The anime aired from February of 1998 to February of 1999 on the Asahi network in Japan. Its forty-seven episodes featured a combination of zany vignettes based on three manga serials: *Miiko* (*kotchi muite miiko*), *Puchan* (*heritako pūchan*), and *Fan Fan Pharmacy* (*fushigi mahō fan fan fāmashī*). For more information, see http://lineup.toei-anim.co.jp/en/tv/mifapu/. Many thanks to George Handlon for bringing this anime to my attention.

3 Satō's name is listed on the album in English-language order and without the macron.

4 For more on Shibuya-kei, see Roberts (2019).

5 Similar dolls appear as band proxies in the music video for Shonen Knife's cover of the Monkees' tune "Daydream Believer."

6 Matthew Gaunt pointed out the price of the bag of banana chips to me.

7 The *I Love Lucy* episode featuring the conveyor-belt scene is called "Job Switching." It aired on September 15, 1952, as season 2, episode 1. https://www.imdb.com/title/tt0609243/, accessed July 28, 2019.

Chapter 7

1 Groups of interest that are not discussed in this chapter include Cibo Matto, Afrirampo, Band-Maid, the Hard Nips, Puffy AmiYumi, the Pat-Pats, the TomBoys, Yellow Machine Gun, 00100, Ichi-Bichi, and many others. Cibo Matto is particularly relevant to the topic of food, given both their name and their first album's focus on the topic. However, their musical aesthetic and approach to food as a lyrical theme are very different from Shonen Knife, and thus I do not discuss them in the main text.

2 Like many songs about consuming food, it is also possible to interpret "Gimme Chocolate" as a metaphor for sex. The double entendre works as both desires for chocolate and for sex begin as a craving staved off until it can no longer be ignored.

3 The band's name is a combination of syllables from each of the member's names and sometimes appears in print as TsuShiMaMiRe.

4 The band members go by their first names only, akin to Shonen Knife. Noodles was originally a four-piece, with Junko on rhythm guitar. She left the band in 2004. See Robson (2010).

5 This can be observed on a fan recording of their SXSW performance. See https://www.youtube.com/watch?v=baBXHqmc-wc.

6 In addition to "After Making Love With Me You Eat Your Wife's Meal," Otoboke Beaver has also recorded another food-related track, "Binge Eating Binge Drinking Bulimia." This track also appears on *Itekoma Hits*.

7 This translation is based on the lyrics published on the official YouTube video from Damnably Records. See https://www.youtube.com/watch?v=dM8N_wcCNbE.

8 For more on theories of the male gaze, see Mulvey (1975).

9 I met with the KCollectors on December 18, 2018, to interview them and attend their show in Tokyo. I met the members of Brinky by coincidence at Shonen Knife's 712 show in Osaka on July 16, 2018. I later communicated with their manager and mother of Risa and Rina, Kawano Maki, via email on June 22 of 2019.

10 Tama-chan was a bit shy at the interview, but kind and hugely capable as a performer.

11 Rina also plays classical cello.

12 There was, however, some raucous moshing and hitting at a Shonen Knife show I attended in Philadelphia in 2015 during their tour with C. J. Ramone. This experience says more about Philly than about the typical atmosphere of Shonen Knife shows.

13 This track was released on Shonen Knife Day (July 12, 2020). Accessed July 12, 2020. https://www.youtube.com/watch?v=qFligovk1DM.

14 Anthony Bourdain, "Brief But Spectacular" (PBS Newshour). Accessed June 29, 2020. https://www.youtube.com/watch?v=AsUSyepx1Ho.

Bibliography

Adorno, Theodor W. "On Popular Music [With the assistance of George Simpson] (1941)." In *Essays on Music*, edited by Richard Leppert, 437–69. Berkeley: University of California Press, 2002.

Ahmed, Sara. "Happy Objects." In *The Affect Theory Reader*, edited by Melissa Gregg and Gregory J. Seigworth, 29–51. Durham: Duke University Press, 2010.

Albala, Ken. "Japanese Food in the Early Modern European Imagination." In *Devouring Japan: Global Perspectives on Japanese Culinary Identity*, edited by Nancy K. Stalker, 35–47. New York: Oxford University Press, 2018.

Allison, Anne. *Permitted and Prohibited Desires: Mothers, Comics, and Censorship in Japan*. Berkeley: University of California Press, 2000.

Aoyama, Tomoko. "Food and Gender in Contemporary Japanese Women's Literature." *U.S.-Japan Women's Journal English Supplement*, no. 17 (1999): 111–36.

Ashkenazi, Michael and Jeanne Jacob. *The Essence of Japanese Cuisine: An Essay on Food and Culture*. Philadelphia: University of Pennsylvania Press, 2000.

Asia Society. *Yoshitomo Nara Nobody's Fool*. 2010. Accessed July 5, 2019. http://sites.asiasociety.org/yoshitomona ra/?_ga=2.243831299.783220428.1582344971 1218581739.1582344971.

Atkins, E. Taylor. *Blue Nippon: Authenticating Jazz in Japan*. Durham: Duke University Press, 2001.

Babymetal Interview. Rock on Range 2015, YouTube. Accessed July 6, 2019. https://www.youtube.com/watch?v=B2F MHwmK9-s.

Bayton, Mavis. *Frock Rock: Women Performing Popular Music*. New York: Oxford University Press, 1998.

Begrand, Adrien. "Deal With It Headbangers—Babymetal is Here." National Public Radio, September 4, 2014. Accessed July 6, 2019. https://www.npr.org/sections/therecord/2014/09/04/345778225/deal-with-it- headbangers-babymetal-is-here.

Biamonte, Nicole. "Triadic Modal and Pentatonic Patterns in Rock Music." *Music Theory Spectrum* 32, no. 2 (Fall 2010): 95–110.

Bolan, David. "SCANDAL Establish Private Record Label 'her.'" JRock News, December 25, 2018. Accessed July 6, 2019. https://jrocknews.com/2018/12/scandal-record-label- her.html.

Bourdaghs, Michael K. *Sayonara Amerika, Sayonara Nippon: A Geopolitical History of J-Pop*. New York: Columbia University Press, 2012.

Bourdain, Anthony. "Brief But Spectacular" (PBS Newshour). Accessed June 29, 2020. https://www.youtube.com/watch?v=AsUSyepx1Ho.

Branstetter, Leah. "The Hidden Histories of 'Fujiyama Mama.'" *Women in Rock & Roll's First Wave*. Accessed July 7, 2019. http://www.womeninrockproject.org/the-hidden-histories-of- fujiyama-mama/.

Butler, Judith. *Gender Trouble: Feminism and the Subversion of Identity*. New York: Routledge, 1990; 2006.

Chocolate and Cocoa Association of Japan. "Japan's History" (*Nihon no rekishi*). Accessed June 16, 2020. http://www.chocolate-cocoa.com/dictionary/history/japan/j01_a.html.

Condry, Ian. *Hip-Hop Japan: Rap and the Paths of Cultural Globalization*. Durham: Duke University Press, 2006.

Cope, Julian. *Japrocksampler: How the Post-War Japanese Blew Their Minds on Rock'n'Roll*. New York: Bloomsbury, 2007.

Covach, John. "Form in Rock Music: A Primer." In *Engaging Music: Essays in Music Analysis*, edited by Deborah Stein, 65–76. New York: Oxford University Press, 2005.

Cwiertka, Katarzyna J. *Modern Japanese Cuisine: Food, Power and National Identity*. London: Reaktion Books, 2006.

Dittmar, Helga, Emma Halliwell, and Suzanne Ive. "Does Barbie Make Girls Want to Be Thin? The Effect of Experimental Exposure to Images of Dolls on the Body Image of 5- to 8-Year-Old Girls." *Developmental Psychology* 42, no. 2 (2006): 283–92.

Dower, John. *Embracing Defeat: Japan in the Wake of World War II*. New York: W.W. Norton & Co., 1999.

Dunn, Kevin. *Global Punk: Resistance and Rebellion in Everyday Life*. New York: Bloomsbury, 2016.

Fujimoto, Dennis. "Barbara Funamura, Creator of Spam Musubi, Dies at 78." Nichi Bei, June 9, 2016. Accessed July 18, 2019. https://www.nichibei.org/2016/06/barbara-funamura creator-of-spam-musubi-dies-at-78/.

Fujimura-Fanselow, Kumiko. "Women's Participation in Higher Education in Japan." *Comparative Education Review* 29, no. 4 (November 1985): 471–89.

Fukutomi, Satomi. "Rāmen Connoisseurs: Class, Gender, and the Internet." In *Japanese Foodways, Past and Present*, edited by Eric C. Rath and Stephanie Assmann, 257–74. Urbana: University of Illinois Press, 2010.

Galbraith, Patrick W. and Jason G. Karlin. *AKB48*. New York: Bloomsbury Academic, 2019.

Galliano, Luciana. *Yōgaku: Japanese Music in the 20th Century*. Translated by Martin Mayes. Lanham: Scarecrow Press, 2002.

Garofalo, Reebee. "Whose World, What Beat: The Transnational Music Industry, Identity, and Cultural Imperialism." *The World of Music* 35, no. 2 (1993): 16–32.

"GIRLS: Runaways-inspired Japanese band cover 'Cherry Bomb,' Blondie, Ramones, KISS and more, 1977." Accessed July 19, 2019. https://dangerousminds.net/comments/girls_runaways_inspired_japanese_band_cover_cherry_bomb_blondie_ramones_kis.

Godoy, Maria. "Ramen Rock: These Punk Legends Sing About Food." National Public Radio, May 25, 2017. Accessed July 12, 2019. https://www.npr.org/sections/thesalt/2017/05/25/529563157/ramen-rock these-japanese- punk-legends-sing-about-food.

Handlon, George. "The Shonen Knife Nexus News." *The Shonen Knife* Nexus 1 (Summer 1998): 7–8.

Hensley, J. J. "Chasing the Knife in the Sky." *Pitch Weekly*, May 8–14, 1997.

Horiguchi, Noriko. "The Devouring Empire: Food and Memory in Hayashi Fumiko's Wartime Narratives and Naruse Mikio's Films." In *Devouring Japan: Global Perspectives on Japanese Culinary Identity*, edited by Nancy K. Stalker, 242–57. New York: Oxford University Press, 2018.

Horkheimer, Max and Theodor W. Adorno. "Culture Industry: Enlightenment as Mass Deception." In *Dialectic of Enlightenment: Philosophical Fragments*, edited by Gunzelin Schmidd Noer, translated by Edmund Jephcott, 94–136. Stanford: Stanford University Press, 2002.

Hosokawa, Shuhei. "Soy Sauce Music: Haruomi Hosono and Japanese Self-Orientalism." In *Widening the Horizon: Exoticism in Post-War Popular Music*, edited by Philip Hayward, 114–44. Bloomington: University of Indiana Press, 1999.

Ishige, Naomichi. "The History and Culture of Food and Drink in Asia: Japan." In *The Cambridge World History of Food*, volume II, edited by Kenneth F. Kiple and Kriemhild Coneè Ornelas, 1175–82. Cambridge: Cambridge University Press, 2000.

Ishihara Motohisa. "Shonen Knife: All the Same, I Wonder if We're a Fad" (Shōnen Naifu yappari watashitachi wa mīhā kana). *G-Scope: Kansai Chaos Guide* 6 (October 1993): 4–6.

Ivy, Marilyn. "The Art of Cute Little Things: Nara Yoshitomo's Parapolitics." *Mechademia* 5 (2010): 3–29.

Jackson, Wanda with Scott B. Bomar. *Every Night is Saturday Night: A Country Girl's Journey to the Rock & Roll Hall of Fame.* [United States]: BMG, 2017. Kindle.

Jagota, Vrinda. "Anata watashi daita ato no yome no meshi." *Pitchfork Review*, February 25, 2018. Accessed July 7, 2019. https://pitchfork.com/reviews/tracks/otoboke-beaver-ana ta- watashi-daita-ato-yome-nomeshi/.

Jones, Jay. "In Hawaii, It's Spam Morning, Noon, and Night." *Dallas Morning News*, March, 2014. Accessed July 18, 2019. https://www.dallasnews.com/life/travel/2014/03/28/in-ha waii-its- spam-morning-noon-and-night.

Kano, Ayako. *Japanese Feminist Debates: A Century of Contention on Sex, Love, and Labor*. Honolulu: University of Hawaii Press, 2016.

Kearney, Mary Celeste. *Gender and Rock*. New York: Oxford University Press, 2017.

Kelly, Kim. "106 Babymetal, 'Gimme Chocolate!!'" *The 200 Greatest Songs by 21st Century Women+*, National Public Radio, July 30, 2018. Accessed July 6, 2019. https://www.npr.org/2018/07/30/627396402/turning-the-tables-the-200-greatest-songs by-21st-century-women-part-5.

Kitagawa Junko. "Teacher Training and Gender" (Kyōin yōsei to jendā). *Japanese Journal of Music Education Practice* 11, no. 1 (2013): 48–55.

Koikari, Mire. "'LOVE! SPAM!' Food, Military, and Empire in Post-World War II Okinawa." In *Devouring Japan: Global Perspectives on Japanese Culinary Identity*, edited by Nancy K. Stalker, 171–86. New York: Oxford University Press, 2018.

Lauden, Rachel. *The Food of Paradise: Exploring Hawaii's Culinary Heritage*. Honolulu: University of Hawaii Press, 1996.

Leonard, Marion. *Gender in the Music Industry: Rock, Discourse and Girl Power*. Burlington: Ashgate, 2007.

Lim, Gerrie, Lee Chung Horn, and Ben Harrison. "Shonen Babes: The Shonen Knife Interview." *Big-O Magazine* (February 1997): 20–5.

Manabe, Noriko. "Globalization and Japanese Creativity: Adaptations of Japanese Language to Rap." *Ethnomusicology* 50, no. 1 (Winter 2006): 1–36.

Manabe, Noriko. "Western Music in Japan: The Evolution of Styles in Children's Songs, Hip-Hop, and Other Genres." PhD diss., City University of New York, 2009.

Matsue, Jennifer Milioto. *Making Music In Japan's Underground: The Tokyo Hardcore Scene*. New York: Taylor Francis/Routledge, 2009.

McClary, Susan. *Feminine Endings: Music, Gender, and Sexuality*. Minneapolis: University of Minnesota Press, 1991.

Middleton, Richard. "'Play it Again Sam': Some Notes on the Productivity of Repetition in Popular Music." *Popular Music* 3 (1983): 235–70.

Ministry of Agriculture, Forestry, and Fisheries. "What is Shokuiku (Food Education)?" Accessed June 22, 2020. https://www.maff.go.jp/e/pdf/shokuiku.pdf.

Mulvey, Laura. "Visual Pleasure and Narrative Cinema." *Screen* 16, issue 3 (Autumn 1975): 6–18.

Nadeshico Sushi. "About Nadeshico." Accessed July 18, 2019. http://www.nadeshico-sushi.com.

Nara Yoshitomo. "Half a Lifetime (Presumably)" (Hansei kari). *Eureka Poetry and Criticism* 49–13, no. 706 (2017): 232–55.

Nara Yoshitomo. "Nobody's Fool." In *Yoshitomo Nara: The Complete Works*, translated by Charles Worthen, 42–5. San Francisco: Chronicle Books, 2011.

Nara Yoshitomo. *Yoshitomo Nara: Lullaby Supermarket*. Translated by Charles Worthen. Nürnberg: Verlag für moderne Kunst Nürnberg, 2001.

Nara Yoshitomo and Stephen Trescher. "My Superficiality is Only a Game: A Conversation between Stephen Trescher and Yoshitomo Nara." In *Yoshitomo Nara: Lullaby Supermarket*, translated by Charles Worthen, 103–7. Nürnberg: Verlag für moderne Kunst Nürnberg, 2001.

Novak, David. *Japanoise: Music at the Edge of Circulation*. Durham: Duke University Press, 2013.

Ohnuki-Tierney, Emiko. *Rice as Self: Japanese Identities through Time*. Princeton: Princeton University Press, 1993.

Plourde, Lorraine. "Babymetal and the Ambivalence of Cuteness." *International Journal of Cultural Studies* 2, no. 3 (2018): 293–307.

Pollack, Andrew. "Barbie's Journey in Japan." *New York Times*, December 22, 1996. Accessed July 9, 2019. https://www.nytimes.com/1996/12/22/weekinreview/barbie-s-journey-in japan.html.

Pope, Edgar W. "Songs of Empire: Continental Asia in Japanese Wartime Popular Music." PhD diss., University of Washington, 1993.

Proust, Marcel. *In Search of Lost Time Volume VI: Time Regained*. Translated by Andreas Mayor and Terence Kilmartin, revised by D. J. Enright. New York: Modern Library, 2003.

Rath, Eric C. "The Invention of Local Food." In *The Globalization of Asian Cuisines: Transnational Networks and Culinary Contact Zones*, edited by James Farrer, 145–64. New York: Palgrave Macmillan, 2015.

Rath, Eric C. *Japan's Cuisines: Food, Place and Identity*. London: Reaktion Books, 2016.

Reddington, Helen. *The Lost Women of Rock Music: Female Musicians in the Punk Era*. Burlington: Ashgate, 2007.

Rhoads, Sean and Brooke McCorkle. *Japan's Green Monsters: Environmental Commentary in Kaijū Cinema*. Jefferson: McFarland Press, 2018.

Roberts, Martin. *Cornelius's Fantasma*. New York: Bloomsbury Academic, 2019.

Robson, Daniel. "Noodles Stir Up Instant Indie Rock on Latest Album." *The Japan Times*, September 17, 2010. Accessed July 6, 2019. https://www.japantimes.co.jp/culture/2010/09/17/music/noodles-stir-up-instant-indie- rock-on-latest-album/#.XSDcS3t7IsM.

Said, Edward. *Orientalism*. New York: Vintage Books, 1979.

Sheng, Annie. "Forging Ahead with Bread: Nationalism, Networks and Narratives of Progress and Modernity in Japan." In *Feeding Japan: The Cultural and Political Issues of Dependency and Risk*, edited by Andreas Niehaus and Tine Walravens, 191–224. Cham: Palgrave Macmillan, 2017.

Shonen Knife Land. Translated by Carl Freire. Tokyo: Little More Company, Ltd., 1998.

Show-ya. "Biography." Show-ya Official Site. Accessed July 19, 2019. http://show- ya.jp/biography/.

Smith, Andrew. TsuShiMaMiRe Interview, October 6, 2010, J-Pop World: The Interview Website for Japanese Musicians and Related Artists. Accessed July 6, 2019. http://www.j- popworld.com/Interviews/TsuShiMaMiRe.php.

Stalker, Nancy K. *Japan: History and Culture from Classical to Cool*. Berkeley: University of California Press, 2018.

Sterling, Marvin. *Babylon East: Performing Dancehall, Roots Reggae, and Rastafari in Japan*. Durham: Duke University Press, 2010.

Sullivan, Denise. *Rip It Up!: Rock 'n' Roll Rulebreakers*. San Francisco: Backbeat Books, 2001.

Tanaka Yasufumi. "Shonen Knife: Japanese Artists with Bill Gates's Certification!?" (Shōnen Naifu: Biru Getsu no osumitsuki!? No nihonjin a-chisuto). *Weekly Ascii*, June 18, 1998, 19.

Tawara Machi. *Salad Anniversary* (*Sarada kinenbi*). Translated by Julie Winters Carpenter. London: Pushkin Press, 2015.

Taylor, Timothy. *Global Pop: World Music, World Markets*. New York: Routledge, 1997.

Tenko. "Biography" Tenko Official Site, 2009. Accessed July 19, 2019. http://tenko-voice.com/en- biography/.

Toei Animation. "Mii fa pū." Accessed June 22, 2020. http://lineup.toeianim.co.jp/en/tv/mifapu/.

Trescher, Stephen. "A Portrait of the Artist as a Young Dog." In *Yoshitomo Nara: Lullaby Supermarket*, translated by Rosanne Altstatt, 9–17. Nürnberg: Verlag für moderne Kunst Nürnberg, 2001.

Wild, David. "Shonen Knife: Cuts Like a Knife." *Rolling Stone*, April 15, 1993. Accessed June 28, 2019. https://www.rollingstone.com/music/music-news/shonen-knife-cuts-like-a-knife-94526/.

Yano, Christine. *Pink Globalization: Hello Kitty's Trek Across the Pacific*. Durham: Duke University Press, 2013.

Yoshimoto Banana. *Argentine Hag* (Aruzenchin babā). Tokyo: Rockin' On, 2002.

Yoshimoto Banana. *Kitchen* (*Kicchin*). Tokyo: Fukutake Shoten, 1988.

Yoshimoto Banana. *The Life of Daisy* (*Hinagiku no jinsei*). Tokyo: Rockin' On, 2000.

Yoshimoto Banana. "The Line He Draws." In *Yoshitomo Nara: Lullaby Supermarket*, translated by Charles Worthen, 47. Nürnberg: Verlag für moderne Kunst Nürnberg, 2001.

Zara. "I Wanna Eat Choco Bars!!!: Shonen Knife." *Girl Frenzy*, no. 4 (1993): 9.

Zara. "Sexist Shit of the Month: Wasted Paper—What is this Music Press Problem?" *Girl Frenzy*, no. 4 (1993): 10.

Žižek, Slavoj. *Looking Awry: An Introduction to Jacques Lacan through Popular Culture*. Cambridge, MA: MIT Press, 1991.

Interviews and Correspondences

Brinky. Email communication with the author. Tokyo, Japan: June 22, 2019.

Handlon, George "Ojisan." Email communication with the author. United States: November 10, 2018; August 6, 2019.

KCollectors. Interview with the author. Tokyo, Japan: December 16, 2018.

Yamano Naoko. Interview with the author. Osaka, Japan: July 16, 2018.

Yamano Naoko. Email communication with the author. Tokyo, Japan: August 10, 2020; August 14, 2020.

Selected Discography

Shonen Knife Albums

Shonen Knife (1982), *Everyone Have Fun (Minna tanoshiku)*, XA Record, XA-2015, cassette.

Shonen Knife (1983), *Burning Farm*, Zero Records, 0-0783, 8-inch vinyl.

Shonen Knife (1984), *Yama No Attchan*, Zero Records, 0-0584, 8-inch vinyl.

Shonen Knife (1986), *Pretty Little Baka Guy,* Zero Records, O-0686, 8-inch vinyl.

Shonen Knife (1991), *712,* Chico Chica, CRCR-6017, CD.

Shonen Knife (1992), *Let's Knife,* MCA Records, MVCD-3, CD.

Shonen Knife (1993), *Rock Animals,* MCA Records, MVCD-8, CD.

Shonen Knife (1993), *We Are Very Happy You Came*, August Records, Rust 004, 33 1/3 rpm.

Shonen Knife (1996), *Brand New Knife,* MCA Records, MVCD-37, CD.

Shonen Knife (1996), *The Birds and the B-Sides,* Virgin, 724384141424, CD.

Shonen Knife (1997), *It's a New Find,* MCA Records, MCVH-14001, CD.

Shonen Knife (1997), *Super Mix,* MCA Records, MVCD-20002, CD.

Shonen Knife (1997), *Ultra Mix,* Universal, MVCH-19001, CD.

Shonen Knife (1998), *Banana Chips* (Single), Universal, MVCH-12002, CD.

Shonen Knife (1998), *Happy Hour,* Universal Records, UMD 80515, CD.

Shonen Knife (1998) *Happy Hour* (Album Promo), Big Deal, BD 9055, CD.

Shonen Knife (2000), *Strawberry Sound,* Universal, MVCH-29042, CD.

Shonen Knife (2002), *Heavy Songs,* Warner Music Group, WINN-82101, CD.

Shonen Knife (2003), *Candy Rock,* First Aid Network, POCE-2532, CD.

Shonen Knife (2005), *Genki Shock,* P-Vine Records, PCD-25029, CD.

Shonen Knife (2006), *Live in Osaka,* P-Vine Records, PCD-25044, CD.

Shonen Knife (2007), *Fun! Fun! Fun!,* P-Vine Records, PCD-25056, CD.

Shonen Knife (2008), *Super Group,* P-Vine Records, PCD-25086, CD.

Shonen Knife (2010), *Free Time,* P-Vine Records, PCD-25106, CD.

Shonen Knife (2011), *Osaka Ramones,* P-Vine Records, PCD-22349, CD.

Shonen Knife (2012), *Pop Tune,* P-Vine Records, PCD-25144, CD.

Shonen Knife (2014), *Overdrive,* P-Vine Records, PCD-25163, CD.

Shonen Knife (2016), *Adventure,* P-Vine Records, PCD-25196, CD.

Shonen Knife (2017), *Ready! Set! Go!!! Adventure Tour 2017,* Valve Records, V148, CD.

Shonen Knife (2018), *ALIVE! In Osaka,* P-Vine Records, PCD-25251, CD.

Shonen Knife (2019), *Sweet Candy Power,* P-Vine Records, PCD-25276, CD.

Other

Babymetal (2014), *Babymetal*, BMD Fox Records, TFCC-86461, CD.
The Beatles (1970), *Let It Be*, Apple Records, PXS 1, 33 1/3 rpm.
Eagles (1972), *Eagles*, Asylum Records, SD 5054, 33 1/3 rpm.
GIRLS (1977), *Nora neko*, Philips, S-7016, 33 1/3 rpm.
GIRLS (1977), *Punky Kiss*, Philips, S-7027, 33 1/3 rpm.
Jackson, Wanda (1958), *Fujiyama Mama*, Capitol Records, 7P-73, 45 rpm.
Kirishima Noboru and Namiki Michiko (1945), *Ringo no uta/ Soyokaze*, Columbia, A 59, 78 rpm.
Mizutama Shōbōdan (1981), *Otome no inori wa da da da*, Kinniku Bijo, KBR-119, 33 1/3 rpm.
Mizutama Shōbōdan (1985), *Manten ni akai hanabira*, Kinniku Bijo, KBR-120, 33 1/3 rpm.
Noodles (2019), *I'm Not Chic*, King Records, QECD-10009, CD.
Obata Miki (1967), *Hatsukoi no retā*, Union Records, US-527-J, 45 rpm.
Otoboke Beaver (2018), *Anata watashi daita ato yome no meshi*, Damnably, WAV single.
Otoboke Beaver (2019), *Itekoma Hits*, Damnably, DAMNABLY080, CD.
Otoboke Beaver (2020), *Dirty Old Fart Is Waiting for My Reaction*, Damnably, MP3 single.
Perfume (2007), *Fan Service*, Tokuma Japan Communications, TKCA-73158, CD single.
Princess Princess (1987), *Teleportation*, CBS/Sony, 28AH 2182, 33 1/3 rpm.
Princess Princess (1988), *Here We Are*, CBS/Sony, 28AH 5004, 33 1/3 rpm.
Princess Princess (1989), *Diamonds*, CBS/Sony, 07SH-3272, 45 rpm.

Ramones (1976), *Ramones,* Sire, SASD-7520, 33 1/3 rpm.

Sakamoto Kyū (1961), *Ue wo muite arukō/Ano musume no na wa nantenkana,* Toshiba Records, JP-8053, 45 rpm.

Scandal (2018), *Honey,* Epic Records Japan, ESCL-4961, CD.

Show-ya (1986), *Queendom,* Eastworld, WTP-90387, 33 1/3 rpm.

Show-ya (1989), *Outerlimits,* Eastworld, CT32-5540, CD.

Tsushimamire (2000), *Hamburger Set,* Self-released, CD.

Tsushimamire (2007), *Nōmiso shōtokēki,* July Records, JKCA-1037, CD.

Tsushimamire (2008), *Six Mix Girls,* BounDEE, Inc., XQGC-1001, CD.

The Who (1971), *Who's Next,* Track Record, 2408 102, 33 1/3 rpm.

Various Artists (1977), *History of Japanese Popular Songs by Original Masters Postwar,* Victor, SJ-8006-1/8, 33 1/3 rpm, 8 discs.

Various Artists (1989), *Every Band Has a Shonen Knife Who Loves Them,* Giant Records, GRI 6036-2, CD.

Various Artists (1998), *Fuji Rock Festival '98 In Tokyo Live,* Polydor, POCP-7341, CD, 2 discs.

Various Artists (2000), *Japanese Pop Cuties in Swingin' 60s,* Teichiku Records, TECH-25650, CD.

Various Artists (2000), *The Powerpuff Girls—Heroes and Villains: Music Inspired by the Powerpuff Girls,* Cartoon Network and Rhino Records, R2 75848, CD.

Various Artists (2001), *Life Is Delicious,* Bad Music Group/Delicious Label, BUMP-006, CD.

Various Artists (2009), *Nippon Girls: Japanese Pop, Beat, and Bossa Nova 1966–70,* Big Beat Records, CDWIKD, CD.

Various Artists (2018), *Dr. Demento Covered in Punk,* Demented Punk Records, DPLP 001, 33 1/3 rpm.

The Velvet Underground (1967), *The Velvet Underground and Nico,* Verve Records, V-5008, 33 1/3 rpm.

Index

Adorno, Theodor W.   88
"After Making Love With Me, You Eat Your Wife's Meal"   111–15
Ahmed, Sara   34–5
AKB48   23, 105
Allison, Anne   31
Anime   3, 31, 68, 74, 91, 100–1, 106–7, 135 n.2
"Apple Song, The"   39–40

Babymetal   58, 103–7
Beatles, The   3, 17, 25, 47–8, 58, 62, 87, 113, 128 n.4
Beavis and Butt-head   54
Benatar, Pat   2
Black Flag   7–8
Blondie   2, 21
BMX Bandits   54
Boogie-woogie   15, 40
Bourdaghs, Michael K.   3, 16–17, 38–9, 41, 128 n.2, 134 n.9
Bourdain, Anthony   124
Breeders, The   2, 109
Brinky   103, 116–18, 136 n.9
Budoōkan   24–5, 116, 129 n.13
Bukimi   69

"Cherry Bomb"   20–1, 129 n.8
Coachella   110
Cobain, Kurt   4

"Daydream Believer"   66, 135 n.5
Dead Kennedys   8
"Diamonds"   25
"Dirty Old Fart is Waiting for My Reaction"   110
DIY   8–9, 68–70
Dunn, Kevin   8–9

Enka   15, 38

5678s, The   111, 128 n.6, 129 n.7
Food
   Chocolate   10, 57–8, 61, 74, 82–3, 86, 90, 100, 105, 131 n.8
   Gyōza   74, 79–81, 86
   Kabosu   118
   Man   38, 79
   Okonomiyaki   30
   Ramen   27, 30, 38, 79, 113, 117
   Rice   36, 62, 73–4, 76, 112, 124

Sushi   38, 66, 73–9, 86, 104, 134 nn.5–6
Takoyaki   30, 112
Franklin, Aretha   15
Fuji Rock   66, 90

Gender   7, 11, 14–15, 19, 30–5, 43, 56, 70, 72, 77–8, 106, 113–14, 119
"Gimme Chocolate"   58, 105, 136 n.2
GIRLS   20–1, 26
Girls Band   13–14
Go-Go's, The   2, 19, 78
Gordon, Kim   2
Group Sounds   3, 17, 18

Handlon, George "Ojisan"   116, 135 n.2
Happy Object   34–5, 58, 124
Hello Kitty   33–4
"Hot Donuts"   118
"Hyper Sweet Power"   108

Idol   9, 18–19, 23–5, 48, 103–4, 111, 113, 129 n.11
Ishizuka Naru   121, 130 n.1
Ivy, Marilyn   68–9

Jackson, Wanda   16
Josei Rock   13–16, 18–23, 26, 42, 72, 103–4, 106–7, 110, 116, 129 n.7

Kakkoii   6
Kano, Ayako   20, 31
Kawaii   6, 40, 69, 104, 106, 110–11, 119, 122, 130 n.6
Kawano Risa   117–18, 120–1
Kayōkyoku   39–41
KCollectors   103, 116–17, 128 n.4, 136 n.9

Lacan, Jacques   59
Late Show With Conan O'Brien, The   54
Licca   46
"Limited Lovers" (Genkai Lovers)   23–4
Lollapalooza   5
L7   5

McClary, Susan   32–3, 95
Manga   3, 67–8
"Minnesota Egg Seller"   40–1
Misora Hibari   15–16
Mizutama Shōbōdan (Polka Dot Fire Brigade)   21–2, 26
Moore, Thurston   4–5, 131 n.3
Morimoto Emi   110, 130 n.1
MTV   5, 32–3, 54
Mudhoney   55
Murakami Takashi   67

Nakanishi Etsuko   130 n.1
Nakatani Michie   3, 8, 32, 52–3, 65–6, 71, 95, 99, 129 n.1

Nara Yoshitomo   67–72, 95–6, 101, 109
Nirvana   4, 30, 55, 86, 92
Nishimura Mana   129 n.1
Noodles (band)   70, 103, 109–10

Obata Miki   17
Olympics   25
Orientalism   80–1, 134 n.9
Osaka   9, 54–5, 65–6, 68, 79, 90, 106, 109–12, 117, 118, 121–2
Otoboke Beaver   103, 110–15, 128 n.6, 136 n.6

Pinky Chicks   17–18
Powerpuff Girls, The   1, 2, 71, 96, 100, 108, 125
Presidents of the United States, The (band)   78
Presley, Elvis   15–17, 41, 51
Princess Princess   14, 22, 24–6, 116
Punk   2–3, 6–9, 18, 21, 26–7, 34, 37, 47, 49, 53, 57, 67–70, 81, 92, 103, 107–8, 110, 112, 115, 118, 120, 122, 124–5

Ramones, The   3, 7, 21, 35, 47, 70, 87, 127 n.1
Red Kross   5

Riot Grrrl   10, 34
Rockabilly   15–17
Rolling Stone   3, 6
Runaways, The   19–21

Said, Edward   80
Sakamoto Kyū   41–2
Scandal (band)   103, 106–7, 109
Second World War   22, 39, 54, 73, 79
Shokuiku   76
Shonen Knife Songs
  "All You Can Eat"   59, 61–2
  "Banana Chips"   54, 66, 87–101
  "Banana Fish"   52, 130 n.3
  "Banana Leaf"   130 n.3
  "BBQ Party"   59–61, 120
  "Better"   123
  "Black Bass"   127, n.7, 130 n.3
  "Blue Oyster Cult"   35
  "Boogie Monster"   7
  "Buttercup (I'm a Super Girl)"   2, 108
  "Butterfly Boy"   5
  "Cannibal Papaya"   5, 35, 52–4, 131 n.3
  "Catch Your Bus"   85
  "Cobra *vs.* Mongoose"   131 n.6

"Cookie Day" 66, 74–5, 82–6, 90
"Deer Biscuits" 130 n.3
"Diet Run" 45–7, 49–52
"Dizzy" 131 n.1, 132 n.12
"Dogfight" 130 n.2
"Dolly" 66
"Elephant Pao Pao" 52
"Flying Jelly Attack" 53
"Fortune Cookie" 119
"Green Tangerine" 27, 118
"Gyoza" 74, 79–81, 86
"Heavy Song" 45–7, 51–2, 105
"Huge Snail" 66
"Ice Cream Cookie Sandwiches" 119–20, 122
"I Wanna Eat Chocobars" 27, 57–8, 90, 105
"Monster Jellyfish" 130 n.3
"People Traps" 66
"Ramen Rock" 27, 117
"Ramones Forever" 3
"Riding on the Rocket" 117
"Rock 'n' Roll Cake" 119
"Shonen Knife" 7
"Strawberry Cream Puff" 58–9
"Sushi Bar Song" 74–9, 86
"Sweet Candy Power" 117, 119–22
"Tomato Head" 5, 52, 54–6, 90
"Twist Barbie" 46–8
"Wasabi" 119
"White Flag" 7–8
Showa-ya 22–4, 25–6
Sonic Youth 4–5
South By Southwest (SXSW) 106, 109–10
Sub Pop 4, 127 n.4
"Sukiyaki" (Ue o muite arukō) 42

Taneda Ritsuko 60, 121, 130 n.1
Tawara Machi 32
Tharpe, Sister Rosetta 15
Three Girls (*Sannin Musume*) 16–17
Tokyo 9, 24–5, 34, 36, 38, 57, 68, 107, 109, 116
Tom Tom Club 7
Transnational 38, 57–8, 73–4, 77–8, 82, 85, 121
Tsushimamire 103, 107–8, 136 n.3

Yamada Kōsaku 84
Yamano Atsuko 3, 8–9, 17, 24, 65, 71, 95, 99, 121

Yamano Naoko 3, 6, 8–10, 27, 30, 32, 46–7, 50–2, 54–5, 57–8, 60–1, 65–6, 71, 75, 78, 81, 83–5, 91–3, 95, 99–101, 118, 120–4

Yano, Christine 33–5

Yellow Magic Orchestra 16, 134 n.9

Yoshimoto Banana 32, 67, 124